Stage Rigging Handbook

Jay O. Glerum

Southern Illinois University Press
Carbondale and Edwardsville

Library of Congress Cataloging-in-Publication Data

Glerum, Jay O.
  Stage rigging handbook.

  Bibliography: p.
  1. Stage machinery—Handbooks, manuals, etc.
2. Stage management—Handbooks, manuals, etc.
3. Theatres—Safety measures—Handbooks, manuals, etc.
4. Theatres—Stage setting and scenery—Handbooks,
manuals, etc.   I. Title.
PN2091.M3G54   1987   792'.025   86-13834
ISBN 0-8093-1318-9 (pbk.)

The paper used in this publication meets the minimum requirements of American
National Standard for Information Sciences – Permanence of Paper for Printed
Library Materials, ANSI Z39.48-1984. ∞™

Contents

Preface

The single greatest cause of rigging accidents in the American theatre is operator error. While some of this error is due to carelessness, much of it is due to lack of knowledge about rigging systems and their safe operation.

Stage Rigging Handbook is intended as a source of written information on the care and safe use of stage rigging equipment. It is hoped that its availability will help to reduce operator error-related accidents, thereby making the theatre a safer place to work.

This book could not have been written without the knowledge so generously shared by the people with whom I have worked.

I wish to thank Charlie Ford and Jim Waring of Catholic University; "Tyke" Lounsbury, John Ashby Conway, and the late Lance Davis of the University of Washington; Floyd Hart and the stagehands of Local 15, IATSE in Seattle; the stagehands of Local 18, IATSE in Milwaukee; and all the road crews with whom I worked over the years.

I would also like to thank my colleagues in the stage rigging industry, especially those at the Peter Albrecht Corporation: Paul Birkle, President; the engineers and staff members.

The words could never have been put into print without the understanding, encouragement, and help of my family, particularly my wife, Sallie.

For permission to quote from the *Wire Rope Users Manual,* 2d ed., I thank the American Iron and Steel Institute. I also thank the United States Institute for Theatre Technology for allowing me to reprint their *Recommended Guidelines for Stage Rigging and Stage Machinery Specifications and Practices.* For permission to reproduce a number of the illustrations, I gratefully acknowledge the Peter Albrecht Corporation, the Macwhyte Company, and the American Iron and Steel Institute. And for illustration reproduction, I thank Wes Jenkins.

Stage Rigging Handbook

Part 1   Hemp Rigging

1.01   Introduction

Hemp rigging is the simplest and oldest form of stage rigging. Although the word "hemp" is actually a misnomer, the term *hemp rigging* generally refers to any natural fiber rope used for attaching, supporting, or flying stage effects.

This type of rigging has been in use since Western theatre was founded by the ancient Greeks as a part of their religious festivals. Some of the plays of Aeschylus, Euripides, and Aristophanes require characters to fly through the air. Since these theatres were open to the sky and had no grids, this effect was accomplished by a device called the "machina." Because the most commonly flown characters were gods, the device became known later as the "deus ex machina"—God in the machine.

The "machina" was a device consisting of a rope drawn through a series of pulleys which were mounted on a pivoting boom. The boom, in turn, was mounted on top of the "skena"—or stage house. A person or object could be lifted from, or lowered onto, the stage by stagehands working the offstage end of the rope. The boom could be rotated to move the flown object on or offstage.

It is generally believed that the technology that made this possible was adapted from that used by Greek sailors. Then, as now, rigging required a good knowledge of the care and use of rope, as well as the ability to tie knots properly.

Today's theatres are generally enclosed structures; many of them have grids; many of them have complex, sophisticated systems for flying stage effects. But still commonly found in use is the simple technique of fastening an object to a rope, running the rope through pulleys, and raising the object into the air. There are many variations and combinations of hemp-rigging systems, but hemp remains as the most basic of all stage rigging. To be a competent stage technician, it is essential to know the correct use of hemp rigging.

1.02   The Hemp Systems

A. Single Line System

The simplest system consists of a single rope, a head block, a loft block, a load (something to fly), and a place to tie off the rope (fig. 1).

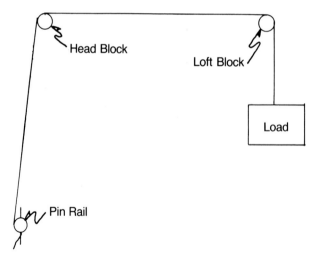

Head Block

Loft Block

Load

Pin Rail

1. Single line hemp set

Rope.   The rope has two ends: the *load end* which is usually onstage; and the *hauling end* which is usually offstage. ½″, ⅝″, or ¾″ no. 1 grade Manila rope is preferred.

Head block. The first pulley that the rope passes through, after leaving the flyman's hands, is called the head block. Usually the head block is offstage of the load. (See section 1.04.B.)

Loft block. The pulley that the rope passes through, directly above the load, is the loft block. It is usually onstage, and is associated with multi-line systems. (See section 1.04.C.)

Spot block. A loft block that is easily movable and can be "spotted," or placed anywhere on the grid, is called a spot block. (See section 1.04.D.)

Pin rail. A rail with vertical pins of wood or metal used for tying off the hauling end of hemp systems is known as the pin rail. (See section 1.05.)

B. Multiple Line System

Two or more lines attached to the same load comprise a multiple line system. The ropes pass from offstage, through a multi-sheave head block (see section 1.04), to individual loft or spot blocks and down to a batten or other object (fig. 2).

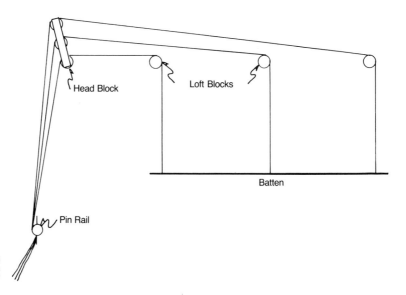

Head Block

Loft Blocks

Batten

Pin Rail

2. Multiple line hemp set

Batten. A pipe or wood rail attached to two or more lift lines of a rigging system is called a "batten." Loads are attached to the battens. Wood and pipe battens are attached to the hemp lines with a clove hitch and two half hitches (fig. 3).

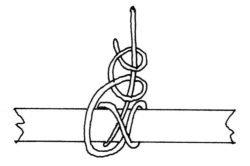

3. Tying hemp to a batten

Lift line identification. The lift lines on a multiple line rigging system are identified with reference to their length from the head block. The line nearest the head block is called the *short line;* the one farther away, the *long line* (fig. 4).

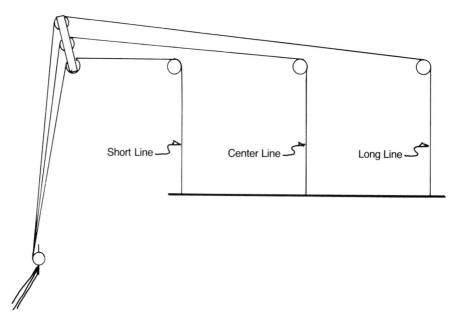

Short Line

Center Line

Long Line

4. Hemp set lift line identification

Always starting from the loft block closest to the head block, typical line designations are as follows:

4-line set: Short, short-center, long-center, long.
6-line set: short-short, short, short-center, long-center, long, long-long.

C. Sandbag Attachment as Counterweight

If the load is too heavy for a single flyman to move, sandbags may be attached to the hauling line. The sandbags are attached by using either a loop of steel cable called a "sunday" (fig. 5) or a trim clamp (fig. 6). (See section 1.06.)

5. Sandbag on a sunday

6. Sandbag on a trim clamp

1.03   Hemp—The Rope

Rope rigging in the theatre is generally referred to as "hemp rigging." There are several types of natural fiber rope that are casually referred to as "hemp." This practice is confusing, since Manila, not hemp, is the preferred type of rope for stage rigging.

Rope can be made in several different ways. Manila rope is almost always twisted, while braiding is commonly used for cotton or synthetic rope. The twisting can be done with either 3 or 4 strands, and the direction of fiber, yarn, and strand twists can vary as well. Different twist directions produce different characteristics in the rope.

The method of twisting for stage use is as follows: the fibers are twisted to the right, or clockwise, into *yarn.* Several pieces of yarn are then twisted to the left, or counter clockwise, and made into *strands.* Three strands are twisted to the right, clockwise, to make a *rope.* This is called a "regular-lay" or "right-lay" rope.

A. Types of Natural Fiber Rope

The three most common types of natural fiber rope come from different sources.

Manila is a hard fiber made from the leaf fiber of the abaca plant. To add to the confusion, it is sometimes called "Manila hemp." It possesses the best combination of the desired characteristics for rigging, of which the most important are strength, cohesiveness, and pliability.

Hemp is a soft fiber made from the inner bark of the main stalk of the cannabis plant. Partly because of the other uses of the leaves of the cannabis, this rope is not readily available in the United States. It is not as strong as Manila.

Sisal is made from the leaf fiber of the agave plant. It is more flexible than Manila but not as strong. It is readily available, less expensive, and easy for the untrained to confuse with Manila. Because it is often used for decorative purposes in the theatre, it is good practice to *clearly mark it* and *store it separately* from rigging rope to prevent it from ever being accidentally used for a rigging job.

When purchasing new rope for rigging, specify the *best grade* of Manila available and ask for the test reports certifying its strength.

B. Strength and Safe Working Load

1. Tensile Strength or Breaking Strength

This means the amount of stress required to break the rope. The breaking strength of rope should be furnished to you by the distributor who supplies the rope. Tests should have been conducted and certified by the manufacturer. The chart of rope specifications compiled by the Cordage Institute is an example of the type of information available. The actual breaking strength may vary slightly from manufacturer to manufacturer (fig. 7).

diameter	new rope tensile strength	safety factor	working load
3/16	406	10	41
1/4	540	10	54
5/16	900	10	90
3/8	1220	10	122
7/16	1580	9	176
1/2	2380	9	264
9/16	3100	8	388
5/8	3960	8	496
3/4	4860	7	695
13/16	5850	7	835
7/8	6950	7	995
1	8100	7	1160
1 1/16	9450	7	1350
1 1/8	10800	7	1540
1 1/4	12200	7	1740

7. Rope strength chart

7

2. Safety Factors

The allowable safe working load is considerably less than the breaking strength. The standard safety factor of 5 has been used for years in the theatre. That is, a safe working load is ⅕, or 20%, of the breaking strength. This is because the breaking strength is calculated by applying a continuous pull to the rope being tested. In actual usage, when there are dynamic or moving forces on the rope, stress equaling or exceeding the breaking strength may suddenly be applied to the rope. This can happen even though the load being lifted is much less than that of the rated breaking strength. (See section 1.03.B-2c.)

Some of the factors affecting the safe working load are:

a. *The strength reduction caused by the knots.* EVERY KNOT REDUCES THE STRENGTH OF A ROPE, SOME BY AS MUCH AS 50%. (See section 1.03.C.)

b. *Wearing caused by abrasion on the rope.* Rope rubbing on some part of the grid, an improperly sized sheave, or dirt on the rope will cause wear and reduce the breaking strength.

c. *The potential for shock load on the rope.* It is easier to break a piece of string with your hands by jerking than by applying steady or constant force. With stage rigging there is always the chance of a flown piece fouling and a sudden shock load being applied.

d. *The length of the rope.* The longer the rope, the easier it is to break. This is caused in part by the weight of the rope itself being added to the weight of the load.

e. *The type of use.* A dead-hung leg in the wing area has less potential for hurting an actor than a working piece, such as a heavy chandelier over the acting area.

3. Calculating the Safe Working Load

a. *Breaking strength.* Know the breaking strength of the size rope being used. Remember that the breaking strength is calculated for *new* rope, and that as rope ages, the probability of weakening occurs.

b. *Be certain of the weight of the load.* This is called the design load that the rope must lift.

c. *Consider the application and degree of risk to life.*

d. *Consider the strength reduction factors.* These are factors which reduce the ultimate breaking strength of the rope, such as knotting. (See section 1.03.C.).

e. *Consider load increase factors.* These are variable factors that may increase the load above its design limit, such as a curtain absorbing moisture from the atmosphere or distribution of a load on a batten. (See fig. 13.)

f. *Allow a 5 to 1 safety factor as minimum.* 5 to 1 means using 20% of the breaking strength. There are occasions when these should be increased to 10 to 1 ($\frac{1}{10}$ of the breaking strength), or even greater. THIS DECISION IS YOUR RESPONSIBILITY!

g. Calculate as follows:

$$\frac{\text{Breaking Strength} \times \text{Strength Reduction Factors}}{\text{Design Load Limit} \times \text{Load Increase Factor}}$$

A RULE OF THUMB: A quick way of estimating the safe working load based on a 5 to 1 safety factor for Manila rope is as follows: "LOAD IN TONS IS EQUAL TO ROPE DIAMETER IN INCHES SQUARED." Example: $\frac{1}{2}'' = .5 \times .5 = .25$ tons (500 lbs.). From this, it is easy to double the safety factor to 10 to 1 by reducing the load by half.

C. Effects of Knotting

Knotting a rope produces bends in the rope and thereby reduces the breaking strength. The sharper the bend, the less strength, and the greater the damage to the rope. It is interesting to note that under test, the rope will fail next to the knot rather than in the knot itself. A knot should be chosen for its strength, stability, and reduction of injury to the rope. For example, a simple overhand knot, the type that seems to get into the middle of a rope all by itself, can reduce the breaking strength by 75%. If it is left in the rope and stress applied to the rope, a permanent weak spot can develop.

D. Care of Rope

Rope is a tool made from organic substances. In order to perform properly within its design parameters, it must be cared for properly.

1. Balance

A rope made by twisting has a proper amount of twist built into it. If the rope has too much twist it will kink. If it has too little twist, it loses strength. When the twist is just right, the rope is "in balance."

Try to avoid twisting Manila rope while working with it. If it becomes kinked from too much twist, it must be untwisted to restore proper balance. This is commonly known as "taking the assholes out of the rope" in stagehands' jargon. This can be done either by actually twisting the rope in the direction opposite to the final strand twist or, preferably, by hanging it vertically. If the end is allowed to hang free from the grid or fly floor, the excess twist will usually come out by itself. A kink pulled through a confined space, such as a head block or loft block, can permanently damage the rope. If there is too little twist in the rope with strands hanging loose from each other, the rope has probably been damaged and should not be used for rigging.

2. Uncoiling Rope

New rope in a full coil is stiff and has a tendency to stay curled. The proper way to uncoil it is to lay the coil down on its side so the inside end is down near the floor. Begin uncoiling the rope from the inside end, turning it in your hand to remove the excess twist. This method will keep the rope from tangling and kinking.

3. Coiling Rope

When finished working with a rope, coil it properly. *Never coil a Manila rope over your hand and elbow.* This will put excess twist in the rope and cause kinking. Right laid rope should be coiled clockwise or "with the sun." Care should be taken to remove all excess twist. Do this by turning the rope as it is being coiled. If the rope is properly coiled and in balance, no twisting or kinking of individual coils should occur. Rope can be coiled over an open hand, on a pin of the pin rail, or if too long and heavy, flat on the floor. When coiling a rope on the floor, be sure that the top coils don't get larger and fall around the bottom coils. This will cause kinking and tangles the next time you use the rope. If coiling a long length of rope that is to be used again immediately, let it pile up in figure-8 coils. *Do not try to pick up the rope when it is coiled in figure 8's.*

4. Storing Rope

On a fly floor, rope should be dressed or properly coiled and hung on a belaying pin. *Don't leave it lying around on the floor.* It will pick up dirt and is dangerous for the flyman to walk on. (See section 1.03.D-5.) Sometimes rope is stored near, or on, the grid since spot lines must be rigged from there. Provide some method to hang the rope, preferably on pegs so that air can circulate freely through it.

5. Keeping Rope Clean

Grit and dirt work into the fibers of the rope and break them through abrasion. Dust absorbs the dressing put on the rope during manufacturing and dries it out, thus shortening life. When a rope gets dirty, wash it in clear water. Pass it through a tub of water and swish it around until the dirt comes out, or hose it off.

6. Drying Rope Properly after Wetting

Since Manila is an organic substance, it will rot or mildew if stored wet. Hang it loosely where dry air can circulate and dry it thoroughly. Inspect the rope for dryness by untwisting it a bit and touching and smelling the fibers. Wet Manila has a distinctive odor.

7. Protecting Rope from Chemicals

Acidic and alkaline substances will dissolve Manila fibers. Grease and oil destroy the fiber friction that holds rope together. Paint solvent dries out rope.

8. Avoiding Rope Overload

Once a rope is stressed beyond its elastic limit, it does not return to its normal strength. Use the right size rope for the job at hand.

9. Avoiding Sharp Bends and Small Sheaves

A rope tied around a sharp corner of a heavy load can be strained at that point so as to permanently weaken the rope. Pad all sharp corners. When a rope passes around a sheave, it bends as it moves. Be sure that the pulley has a large enough diameter so that the rope won't be severely strained. (See section 1.03.D-10.)

10. Avoiding Abrasion

Don't drag rope over rough surfaces. This will cause unnecessary wear on the rope. Sheaves or pulleys must be grooved for the size rope that is being used. If the groove is too small, the friction on the rope will cause it to wear and weaken. Be sure that blocks are aligned so that the rope does not rub on side plates.

11. Avoiding Shock Loading

Jerking a rope or suddenly dropping a load (such as when a fouled piece of rigging falls free) can easily break a rope. One of the reasons that the safe working load is much less than the breaking strength of a rope is to allow for this possibility. The greater the shock load, the easier it is to break the rope.

12. Adjusting Rope for Humidity

Humidity affects Manila rope. As the humidity increases, the fibers absorb the moisture from the air and swell. The rope gets thicker and shorter. As the humidity drops, the rope dries out; the fibers shrink in diameter and the rope gets longer. In environments where there is significant change in humidity, such as theatres with intermittent air conditioning, or out-of-doors, multiple line hemp sets must be trimmed before every performance. Because the lines are different lengths on multiple line sets, they will not shrink or expand evenly. A hanging drop, level at low humidity, will get high on the long side as the humidity increases. In this case, the load is free to move and no damage will be done to the rope. In some instances, where the load can't move, such as a guy rope, permanent damage to the rope may occur owing to shrinkage caused by dampness. The rope can get stretched past its elastic limit and lose some of its tensile strength. In such cases, it is important to remember to slack off the tension on the rope as it contracts.

13. Inspecting Rope Periodically

Using the rope until it breaks is irresponsible. As you use it, *be aware of it. Look at it!* If something does not feel or look right, replace it, rather than take a chance. Visually, *inspect all rigging rope over its complete length on a regular basis.* This is best accomplished by unrigging it and inspecting, by hand and eye, its entire length. (See section 1.03.E.)

14. Rotating Rope Position

Periodically change around the ropes. Reverse the ends and change the jobs they do. This will avoid causing weak spots and spread the wear throughout the rope.

THINK: All of the above recommendations for taking care of rope are common sense! Take the time to care for the rope. Replacing rope is expensive. Replacing a life is impossible.

E. Indications of Wear

When inspecting a rope, look for the following:

Indentations.   These are caused by a kink being pulled through a block or excess strain of a knot.

Wear.   A rough or worn spot caused by abrasion.

Variation in diameter.   Is the rope a lot thinner than it should be? Has it been overstressed?

Dryness. Are the fibers dry and brittle? Untwist a strand and break a few fibers between your fingers. Overly dry rope will break easily.

Wetness. A wet rope loses a good deal of its strength. If it is wet, *don't use it.* Dry it well before using.

Rot. Untwist it in several places. Look on the inside where the strands touch each other for signs of mildew and rot.

F. Testing a Rope

If you are not sure of the strength of a rope, don't guess. Test it or have it tested. If a nearby college or university engineering school has testing equipment, ask it to run a destructive test on a sample for you. If that is not possible, rig the rope as it is to be used and then load it, from 5 to 10 times the anticipated working load. Remember, the greater the risk of the situation, the greater the safety factor needed. If the rope breaks or stretches to the point of deformation, provide new rope, bigger rope, or both. While this is time-consuming, it is better than having the rope break while it is in use. *Do not keep old unsafe rope around.* Throw it out, or cut it so that it doesn't get used by a person who doesn't know that it is weak.

G. Selecting the Right Rope for the Job

1. For general "hemp" rigging choose no. 1 (or best grade) Manila.

2. Choose the proper diameter rope to hold the expected load and which is compatible with the blocks available for the job. Common sizes of blocks are ½″ and ⅝″. ½″ rope will work quite nicely in ⅝″ sheaves, but ⅝″ rope will be chewed to shreds by ½″ sheaves.

3. Request test reports from your supplier.

4. Whip ends to keep from unraveling. (See section 4.01.A-2.)

5. Uncoil it properly.

6. Safe working loads should be posted backstage in a prominent place so all technicians will have the information available when they need it—while working backstage with the rope.

7. It is good practice to mark various lengths of rope by color-coding the whipped ends, or in some other way. A 125′ rope and a 150′ rope are difficult to distinguish between when coiled up on a dark grid.

8. Periodically inspect all rope and replace it if there are *any* doubts about its condition.

1.04   Blocks

Blocks are pulleys which are used to change the direction of the force which moves a load. A block consists of the following parts (fig. 8): 1) sheave, 2) bearings, 3) shaft or axle, 4) side plates, 5) retainers, 6) mounting device.

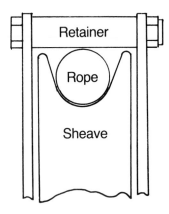

9. Rope sheave

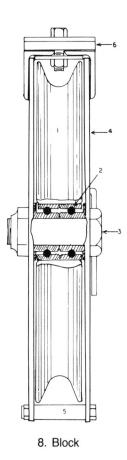

8. Block

1. The *sheave* is a grooved wheel. The groove should be sized to support at least ⅓ of the circumference of the rope. The edges of the groove should be flared enough to allow the rope to enter and exit the groove without abrasion (fig. 9).

As a recommended guideline, the minimum sheave diameter should be 6 times the rope diameter.

2. The *bearings* reduce the friction between the sheave and the shaft. Of the many types of bearings, some require periodic lubrication and some are permanently lubricated and sealed. The sealed bearings may eventually dry and have to be replaced. If the sheave does not turn easily or if it squeaks, there is a bearing problem that should be analyzed and corrected.

3. The *shaft* should be large enough to support the required load. It must be attached to the side plates to prevent the shaft from rotation. All rotational action should be by the sheave.

4. The *side plates,* made of steel, support the shaft. The retainers and other spacers keep the side plates evenly separated.

5. The *retainer* is usually a length of pipe or tubing held in place by a bolt that prevents the rope from jumping out of the sheave groove. Retainers should not be placed too close to the sheave or they will rub on the rope or sheave. They can usually be adjusted slightly by loosening the bolt and moving it closer or farther away from the sheave.

6. The *mounting device* holds the block to the support steel. A block will have a tendency to move in the direction of the resultant force. (See section 1.04.A-1.) The mounting device should provide metal to metal contact. This is especially important in preventing movement in the horizontal direction (fig. 10).

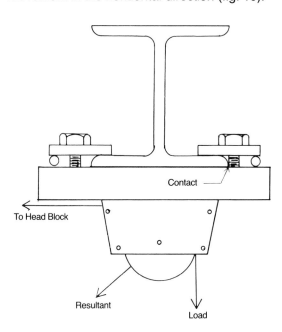

Contact

To Head Block

Resultant

Load

10. Underhung block

A. Loads

In order to calculate the loading it is necessary to understand the forces that are applied to the block.

1. Applied and Resultant Forces

There are two forces applied to a block at any given time: the force of the load and the force that holds or moves the load. These combined forces produce a resultant force (fig. 11).

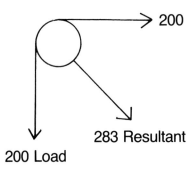

200

283 Resultant

200 Load

11. Applied and resultant force diagram, 90°

The direction of the resultant force is found by bisecting the angle between the two applied forces. The following formulas can be used to help determine the loading. All formulas are based on static loading.

2. Right Angle Formula

A formula for finding the resultant force on a block, when the applied forces are at right angles to each other, is as follows: The square root of twice the load squared.

$\sqrt{2L^2}$ Example: A load of 200 lbs. = 2(200)² =
80,000 = 283 lbs.

16

3. Any Angle Formula

To calculate the resultant force when the applied forces are at an angle other than 90°, it is necessary to determine the weight of the load and the exact angle between the applied forces. It is also necessary to have access to a table of trigonometric functions. (A calculator with the trig function works best.) For example, using a load of 200 lbs. and an angle of 100° (fig. 12), do the following:

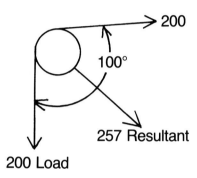

200 Load

12. Applied and resultant force diagram, 100°

    a. Subtract the known angle from 180°
       $180° - 100° = 80°$
    b. Divide the known angle in half
       $100 \div 2 = 50°$
    c. Set up the formula:

$$\frac{\text{Load} \times \sin(180° - \text{known angle})}{\text{Resultant } \sin \frac{\text{known angle}}{2}} =$$

$$\frac{200 \times \sin 80°}{\sin 50°} = \frac{200 \times .985}{.766} - 257 \text{ lbs.}$$

4. Batten Loading

The following table (fig. 13) shows the percentage of the total load that is applied to each loft block and lift line on a batten. These percentages are based on the load being evenly distributed on the batten. When trimming a hemp set, it is possible to feel the difference in weight from line to line.

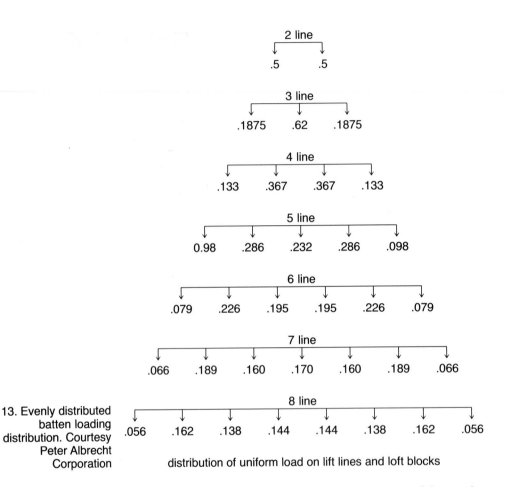

2 line
.5   .5

3 line
.1875   .62   .1875

4 line
.133   .367   .367   .133

5 line
0.98   .286   .232   .286   .098

6 line
.079   .226   .195   .195   .226   .079

7 line
.066   .189   .160   .170   .160   .189   .066

8 line
.056   .162   .138   .144   .144   .138   .162   .056

13. Evenly distributed batten loading distribution. Courtesy Peter Albrecht Corporation

distribution of uniform load on lift lines and loft blocks

On a 3-line set, the end lines each support 18.75% of the total weight, and the center line supports 62.50% of the total weight.

B. Head Blocks

There are two types of head blocks most commonly used for hemp sets. One type has all of the sheaves mounted on a single shaft (fig. 14).

14. Single shaft head block

The other type stacks the sheaves on separate shafts (fig. 15).

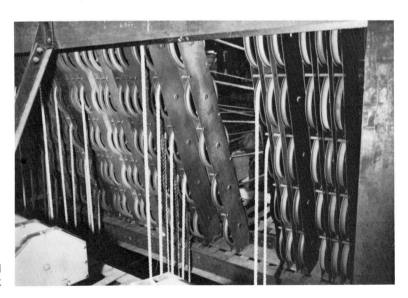

15. Stacked head block

C. Loft Blocks

Loft blocks can either be mounted on the grid or underhung on support steel over the grid (fig. 16).

16. Loft block

D. Spot Blocks

Spot blocks are loft blocks designed to be easily movable. Extreme care must be taken to see that blocks are securely mounted. The V-shaped piece of steel on the underside of the block is designed to fit tightly against the grid steel to prevent horizontal slipping (fig. 17).

17. Spot block

The V shape allows the block to be mounted at an angle to the grid steel in order to maintain a proper fleet angle.

E. Mule Blocks

Mule blocks change the direction of lift lines in the horizontal plane. This type of block is used when it is not possible to run the lift line straight from the head block to the loft block (fig. 18).

18. Mule blocks. Courtesy Peter Albrecht Corporation

F. Idler Pulleys

Idler pulleys are nonload bearing blocks. Their function is to keep the lift lines from sagging on long runs from head blocks to loft blocks. Since an idler pulley does not bear any of the lifting load, it can be of a much lighter construction than a loft or head block (fig. 19).

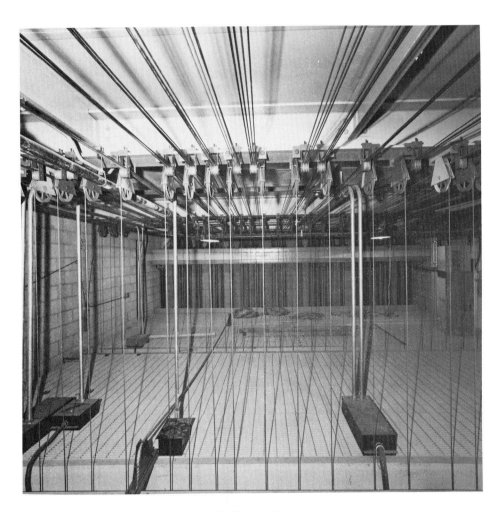

19. Idler pulleys. Courtesy Peter Albrecht Corporation

G. Snatch Blocks

Snatch blocks open so that a lift line can be placed on the sheave without being threaded through from the end. Snatch blocks are handy for muling or idler purposes, after the load has been attached to a lift line (fig. 20).

20. Snatch block

1.05   Pin Rail

The pin rail is used to tie off the hauling end of a hemp system. The rail is a horizontal wooden beam, or large pipe, pierced with vertical pins. The pins are either made of hardwood or pipe. They can be either fixed to the rail or removable.

A. Fixed Pin Rail

As the name implies, the pins are permanently fixed and cannot be removed. This type of rail is safer than the loose pin rail for cinching a load. Another advantage is that the pins cannot be lost.

B. Loose Pin Rail

On this type of rail, the pins are removable. It is possible to release the tie-off by pulling the pin out. The pins can also be removed to clear space for extra large coils of rope hanging on the rail.

C. Single Pin Rail

A single pin rail is, as the name implies, one rail. High and low trim are tied off on adjacent pins.

D. Double Pin Rail

The double pin rail (fig. 21) consists of two rails. The top rail is usually set further onstage than the lower rail.

21. Double pin rail

With this type of pin rail, the low trim is usually tied off on the top rail, and the high trim is tied off on the bottom rail.

E. Tying Off

There is an exact procedure for tying off a hemp line or set.

    1. Take a single wrap around the underside of the pin (fig. 22).

22. Tying off, step 1

The friction of the rope on the pin immediately gives the operator control of the load. It is always better to raise the load a little too high, make the wrap, and then ease it into trim position.

    2. Cross the rope on the face of the rail and take a wrap around the top of the pin (fig. 23).

23. Tying off, step 2

3. Make another wrap around the underside of the pin, in the same direction as the first wrap.

4. Form a loop by twisting the rope. The free end goes under the standing part (fig. 24).

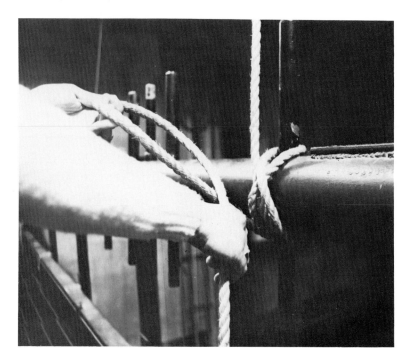

24. Tying off, step 3

5. Put the loop over the top of the pin as shown (fig. 25).

25. Tying off, step 4

Pull it tight (fig. 26).

26. Tying off, step 5

1.06   Sandbags

Sandbags are usually used as counterweight for hemp rigging. They are made of heavy canvas that is reinforced with rope. The rope has a snap hook affixed to it for easy attachment to the lift lines. Sandbags commonly range in size from 10 lbs. to 100 lbs. Sand can be added or removed from the bags in order to match the weight of the load. There should be a container on the fly floor to hold unused sand.

A. Attaching Sandbags with a Sunday

One method of attaching sandbags to the lift line is to use a loop of steel cable, called a "sunday." A piece of ⅛" aircraft cable, 3' to 4' long, is formed into an endless loop, either by using nicopress sleeves or by tying a "sunday knot" in it (fig. 27).

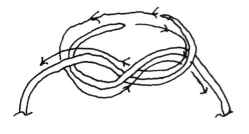

27. Sunday knot

   The sunday is attached to the lift line by wrapping the loop around the lift line and passing one end of the loop through the other (fig. 28).

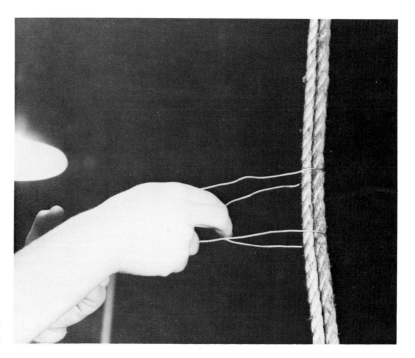

28. Attaching sunday to hemp lines

   The sandbags are then hung on the remaining loop (see fig. 5).

B. Attaching Sandbags with a Trim Clamp

Another method of attaching sandbags to the lift lines is to use a trim clamp. The clamp is bolted over the ropes with a steel loop down. Sometimes it helps to squeeze the trim clamp together, with a C-clamp, when putting it on. There are spring loaded jaws inside the trim clamp that must be compressed in order to tighten the nuts on the trim clamps (fig. 29).

29. Trim clamp

The sandbags are then hung on the loop (see fig. 6).

The advantage of using a trim clamp is that the load may be re-trimmed after the trim clamp and sandbags are attached. This is done by pulling the longest lines through the clamp, thus raising the low points. If there is an unbalanced load, it may be necessary for someone on the stage floor to hold down the flown piece at the high points while the low points are raised. Instead of holding the piece directly, a tailing rope can be tied to the batten at these points. (See section 4.04.C.)

1.07   Spot Line Rigging

Hemp sets can be positioned, or "spotted," for special production needs. Either single or multiple line sets can be used to provide flying capability in positions and patterns to supplement permanently installed batten sets.

A. Positioning Loft Block

The installation of a spot line set begins with positioning the loft block. Usually, the point where the lift line must drop is determined on the stage floor. A target that is easily visible from the grid is placed on the floor. Using a plumb bob, a weight on the lift line, or the "spit method," position the block on the grid directly above the target (or as close as possible). The loft block is then lined up with the drop point over the target, and the sheave is aligned with the head block position. The block is then secured to the grid.

NOTE: It is most important that the block be firmly mounted so that there is no chance of the block slipping. (See section 1.04.D.)

B. Positioning Head Blocks

Once the loft blocks are firmly attached, the head blocks are aligned with the loft blocks and secured in place. It is important that the rope travel in a straight line from head block sheave to the spot block sheave in order to avoid abrasion to the rope. When using the type of head block with the sheaves mounted side by side, it is sometimes necessary to angle the spot blocks slightly (fig. 30).

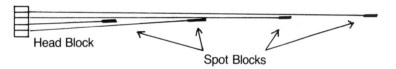

30. Head block-spot block alignment

Head Block

Spot Blocks

C. Running Rope

Once the blocks are positioned, the rope is fed through the blocks from the grid. Attach a weight, or tie off the rope as soon as it is fed through the blocks, to keep it from running away. Storing the rope somewhere near the grid eliminates the necessity of hauling the rope to the grid every time a spot line must be run.

D. Weighting Rope

The onstage end of the rope should be either attached immediately to the load, or weighted. Weighting can be done either with a small sandbag or by running the end of the rope through a short section of pipe (figs. 31, 32).

31. Rope weighted
    with sandbag

32. Rope weighted
    with pipe

34

1.08   Operation of Hemp Rigging

The safe operation of hemp rigging requires a thorough knowledge of how the rigging system works. This knowledge includes knowing the function of each of the components and knowing how the components work together to make an integrated system. In addition to knowing the system, hemp rigging requires more human physical strength to operate than other types of rigging. At times, the operator will need to move unbalanced loads solely by brute strength. Since almost all lift line connections are knots, the operator must also have a thorough knowledge of knot-tying. Both strength and knowledge must be properly applied. Concentration and attention to detail are essential to the safe operation of hemp rigging. In brief:

1. Know the system.
2. Know how it is supposed to work.
3. Concentrate on the task at hand.

A. Safety Inspect All Components

The components of a rigging system should be thoroughly inspected on a periodic basis. The resident technician, house carpenter, or technical director has the responsibility for maintaining the equipment. It is his job to see that the rigging system is in perfect working order. The system should be inspected, component by component, at least once a year! If the resident technician does not have sufficient expertise to conduct an inspection, it will be necessary to hire an expert from a rigging company to do it. (See section 4.08.)

In a strange theatre, it is always necessary to inspect the rigging before attaching loads. It must never be assumed that the rigging is in good condition just because it is there!

Knowing a rigging system goes beyond a knowledge of the parts and their location. Every rigging system has its own feel, sound, and smell. Becoming aware of these sensory perceptions is essential, so that every time the system is used, there will be instant awareness if something is out of the ordinary. A sheave with dry bearings, or a rope rubbing where it shouldn't, makes distinct sounds. They also feel different. A piece of dry rotting hemp, or hemp that has been charred by a lighting instrument, has a distinct smell. Knowing how the system should be when it is in perfect operating condition is a prerequisite to spotting problems.

B. Attaching Loads

Most of the time, loads are attached at the stage-floor level. The flyman should lower the load end of the rope to the stage floor. Before
moving any piece of rigging during a set-in or a strike, always warn
the people onstage and on the grid by yelling "Heads up!" If the
flyman can't see the load, a spotter should be used. The spotter
watches the load and communicates directly with the flyman. Be
sure that the load is within a 5 to 1 safety factor of the rigging system. (For specific information on attaching techniques, see part 4.)

Once the load is attached, it is pulled up to the low trim position.
Several people may be required to raise the load. One competent
person must be designated to tie off the rope. At this point, multiple
line sets are "trimmed." This means that the individual lines are
pulled, in order to level, or "trim," the piece to the stage floor or rele-
vant low trim datum point. The rope is then tied off. On a double
pin-rail system, tie-off is made on the upper pin rail.

With the low trim tied off, the flown piece is then raised to its high
trim position and tied off again. On a two-rail system, use the lower
rail. Use an adjacent pin on a single-rail system. At this point, sandbags are attached and the load is balanced. (Enough weight should
be added to the offstage end to ensure ease of operation. However,
the line set must be slightly "load heavy" in order to operate at all.)
When all sandbags have been attached, the piece should be operated to recheck high and low trim positions.

C. Removing Loads

The first step in removing a lead from a hemp set is to be sure that the stage area under the load is clear.

With the lines tied off at high trim, remove the sandbags and sunday (or trim clamp) from the rope. Untie the low trim. Sort out the rope and be sure that it is free and clear.

Untie the high trim, keeping a sufficient number of wraps around the pin to maintain control as the flown piece is lowered to the stage floor (fig. 33).

33. Letting in an unweighted piece

The friction of the rope, around the pin, acts as a brake. It is good practice to never unwrap the rope completely from the pin until the load is on the floor.

D. Trim Marks

Trim heights on hemp rigging may be marked on the rope by using tape. However, tape can come off or leave a sticky residue when it is removed.

Another method is to use a piece of brightly colored yarn. Untwist the rope slightly and insert a piece of yarn about 6″ long through the rope. As with tape, different colors can be used to indicate different trim positions (fig. 34).

34. Yarn trim mark

E. Lashing with Small Stuff

When tying off high and low trims on different pins, it sometimes helps to use small cord to lash the low trim tie-off in place (fig. 35).

35. Tie-off lashed to pin

Doing this will help keep the lines from fouling on the low trim pins when moving the piece from high to low trim. The small cord also serves as a reminder not to untie the low trim pins.

F. Retrimming

Because of the effect of moisture on Manila rope, changes in humidity affect the trim of hemp rigging. On multiple line sets, the longest ropes change the most. Therefore, trims should always be checked before performance time.

If a multiple line set is out of trim, the sunday must be removed to retrim. This is a time-consuming task, and obviously points to the advantage of using a trim clamp. (See section 1.06.B, fig. 29.) Be sure to check dead-tied sets, as well as those that move.

G. Coiling and Dressing

The extra rope on a fly floor should always be properly coiled and hung on a pin. This is called "dressing" the rope. This prevents the rope getting tangled and dirty from the flymen walking on it.

Keep the fly floor clean, so when rope is placed on the floor, it won't get dirty. (See section 1.03.D.)

H. Showtime Operation

Operating rigging during a performance is very much like stage managing. Most of the work is in the preparation before the performance. Knowing the rigging system, being sure that it is in good, safe condition, properly attaching the loads, clearly setting trim marks, and properly dressing the loose rope on the fly floor all contribute to an organized and reliable performance.

It is good practice to check trim marks and low trim tie-offs before every performance. Be sure the trim marks are still in place. Be sure that tie-offs have not slipped, or that humidity has not changed rope lengths.

When letting a piece in, remove the coiled rope from the pin and lay it on the fly floor. It should be placed where it can't be stood on and thus the rope will uncoil evenly, without tangling.

On the "warn" cue, find the proper rope and review which direction it moves. On the "standby" cue, untie (if it is being let in) or get ready to pull (if it is being taken out). On the "go" cue, move the piece, being sure that either operator or spotter can see the piece and the stage floor under it.

1.09   Operation Summary

1. Know the rigging system.
2. Inspect system thoroughly at regular intervals.
3. Be sure the load does not exceed the safe capacity of the system.
4. Use correct knots for attaching loads and tying off on the pin rail.
5. Maintain visual contact with a moving piece. Use a spotter, if necessary.
6. Warn people on the stage and the grid before moving a flown piece.
7. Maintain control of a moving piece at all times.
8. Wear hand protection.
9. Keep working area clean.

1.10   Safety Inspection Summary

On a regular basis, at least once a year, the rigging system should have a thorough safety inspection. This service can be provided by professional rigging companies for a fee. The inspection should include:

1. Rope: *a*) inspect the entire length of each rope, *b*) inspect the running clearance of each rope.

2. Pin rail: *a*) inspect mounting bolts that hold the rail down, *b*) smooth rough spots on wooden rails.

3. All head and loft blocks: *a*) inspect and tighten mounting clamps, *b*) check support steel for deflection, *c*) check for dry bearings.

4. Sandbags: check for rot, tears, deterioration.

5. Trim clamps and sundays: check general condition.

Part 2 Counterweight Rigging

2.01 Introduction

The invention of counterweight rigging was the next logical step in the progression of flying equipment for the stage. It began to appear in the first quarter of the twentieth century. The early systems employed a rack, or arbor, in which to stack metal weights. This arbor was attached to the hemp lift lines, and a single hand line was attached to the arbor. The shrinking and stretching of the hemp lift lines, because of changes in humidity, still posed a problem. This was solved by using plow steel wire rope for the lift lines. Wire guides gave the arbors some vertical stability. Eventually, "T-bar" guide rails appeared and have become the most common form of guide systems.

For efficiency, the counterweight system is a great improvement over hemp rigging. The onstage load can be counterweighted much faster than bagging a hemp set. The single hand line, wire rope lift lines, and lock rail reduce work and thus save time.

2.02   Single Purchase Counterweight System

A typical single purchase counterweight system (fig. 36) consists of:
1. Head block for lift line and hand line
2. Loft blocks (mule blocks as needed)
3. Wire rope lift lines
4. Batten
5. Hand line, usually ¾" Manila
6. Counterweight arbor
7. Lock rail
8. Tension block
9. T-bar guide rails
10. Loading bridge

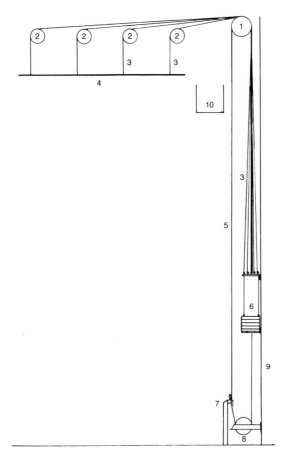

36. Single purchase counterweight set

This system is used when there is clear wall space on one side of the stage from grid height to the stage floor. Counterweights are used in a 1 to 1 ratio. That is, 1 pound of counterweight is needed for each pound of load weight.

2.03   Double Purchase Counterweight System

A double purchase system is used when some obstruction prevents full travel of the arbor from grid to stage floor. Note the compound rigging of both hand line and lift line in figure 37. The batten travels 2 feet for every 1 foot of travel for the arbor. Consequently, 2 pounds of counterweight are required for every 1 pound of load.

The arbors must be sized larger than a single purchase system in order to have the same lifting capacity. Larger arbors often make loading and unloading more difficult and thus more dangerous.

A typical double purchase counterweight system (fig. 37) consists of

1. Head block for lift line and hand line
2. Loft blocks (mule blocks as needed)
3. Wire rope lift lines
4. Batten
5. Hand line, usually ¾" Manila
6. Counterweight arbor
7. Lock rail
8. Tension block
9. T-bar guide rails
10. Loading bridge
11. Arbor blocks
12. Hand line tie-off
13. Hand line and lift line tie-off

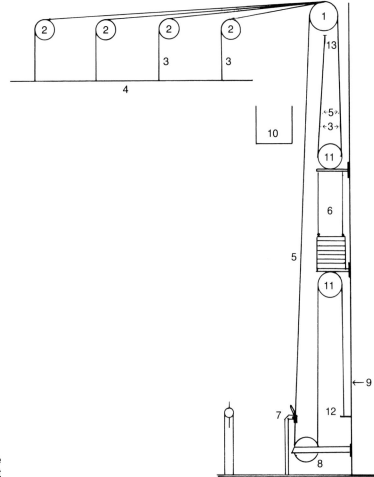

37. Double purchase
counterweight set

2.04   Wire Rope

With the invention of the counterweight rigging system, wire rope replaced hemp as the lift line material. Wire rope is not susceptible to stretching or shrinking from humidity changes, and it is much stronger per unit of cross-sectional area than Manila rope.

A. Types of Wire Rope

There are many types of wire rope. Each of these types has specific properties of strength, flexibility, elasticity, corrosion resistance, rotation resistance, direction of twist, and many other special qualities. The types most commonly used for stage rigging are 7 × 19 galvanized aircraft cable and 6 × 19 improved plow steel. The numbers indicate the number of strands (7) and the number of wires in each strand (19) that make up aircraft cable. With regard to improved plow steel, the numbers indicate 6 strands with 15 through 26 wires in each strand (fig. 38).

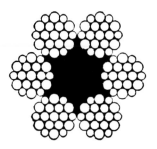

38. Cross section 7 × 19 aircraft cable. Courtesy Macwhyte Company, *Wire Rope Catalog of Tables, Data, and Helpful Information*

As a general rule, the greater the number of wires, the greater the flexibility. (See section 2.05.B.)

B. Strength and Safe Working Load

(See section 1.03.B for formula.) The distributor or manufacturer of the wire rope can provide a table of breaking strength. The safe working load is no less than ⅕ of the breaking strength. Allowing for strength reduction factors and load increase factors, a ⅛ factor is much safer. That is, never load a cable more than ⅛ its rated breaking strength.

C. Attaching to Batten and Arbor

Applying a load to wire rope will cause it to stretch. Even if a batten is evenly loaded, the load on each lift line is not equal. Many loads are not evenly distributed, which adds to the problem of uneven cable stretch. (See section 1.04.A.) Therefore, when terminating the lift lines at arbor and batten, a method of adjustment must be provided. There are several common methods used to attach wire rope to battens.

1. Trim Chain

The wire rope is terminated at the end of a chain using a thimble and clips or nicopress sleeve. In considering the method of terminating the cable, it is good to keep in mind that nicopress sleeves will maintain 100% of the cable breaking strength. Cable clips main-

46

tain 80%. The chain is wrapped around the batten 1½ times and is secured to itself using a shackle, bolt, or Fulton clip. The chain should be sized for the load with an appropriate safety factor. ¼" proof coil chain is the minimum size recommended by chain manufacturers. Snap hooks are often used to secure the chain to itself. These should only be used if they have the proper rating. Bolts, shackles, and Fulton clips can be purchased with the proper rating (figs. 39, 40).

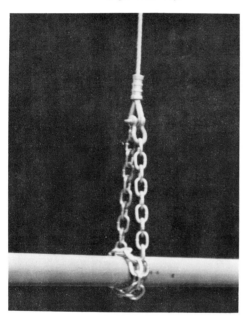 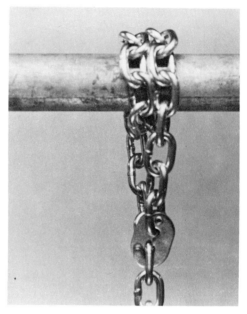

39. Lift line with trim chain attached to batten   40. Trim chain with fulton clip

2. Clove Hitch with Cable Clip

This method works for both temporary and permanent use. The holding is done by the clove hitch. The clip keeps the end of the wire rope from working loose. The clove hitch reduces the strength of the wire rope to about 65% of the ultimate breaking strength. Leveling is done at the arbor end.

3. Turnbuckle

The wire rope can be attached to the eye end of a jaw/eye turnbuckle, using a thimble and clips or nicopress sleeve. The jaw end can then be attached to the arbor or a pipe clamp on the batten. As wire rope runs over a sheave, the twist in the wire rope causes it to

47

turn. Jam nuts, cotter pins through the rod ends, or wire mousing should be used to keep the turnbuckle from turning and separating. All three methods are shown in figure 41.

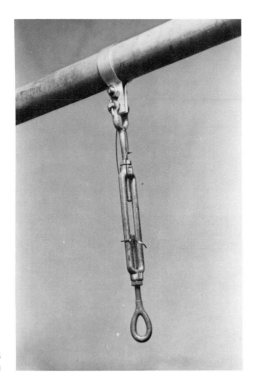

41. Turnbuckle on a batten

Leveling the batten is much easier if the trimming device is attached to the batten rather than to the arbor. The batten is lowered to a point where it is convenient to measure from floor to batten. Measurements are made where each lift line is attached to the batten, and the lines are lengthened or shortened as required. If the adjusting device is on the arbor, then one person onstage must yell to the person adjusting at the arbor. This is often awkward and time-consuming.

D. Indications of Wear

When inspecting the lift lines for signs of wear, look for broken wires, flattened wires, separation in wire or strand, rust, signs of chemical etching or anything unusual. Wire rope in good condition is clean, well formed, and free from dirt, grease, and other discoloration (fig. 42).

42. Signs of wear and misuse. Courtesy American Iron and Steel Institute, *Wire Rope Users Manual*

2.05   Blocks

In this section, characteristics that pertain specifically to wire rope blocks will be discussed. (For general information pertaining to blocks, see section 1.04.)

A. Sizing

When a wire rope is bent over a pulley or drum, each wire that makes up the cable is bent and straightened. This constant bending causes fatigue in the cable. Therefore, proper sheave diameter sizing is far more critical for wire rope than hemp rope. This recommended sheave diameter is a multiple of the wire rope diameter.

The minimum sheave tread diameter for 7 × 19 aircraft wire rope is 30 × the diameter of the wire rope. Using ¼″ for example, .25 × 30 = 7.5″ minimum sheave tread diameter.

The groove of the sheave must also be properly sized for the wire rope. If it is too big, it does not support the wire rope properly and the wire rope will flatten out and lose strength. If the groove is too small, the abrasion of the cable, rubbing the groove walls, will cause wear on both cable and sheave. A tolerance of +.015 to −.00 is acceptable. Using hemp blocks for wire rope is never acceptable.

B. Head Blocks

The head blocks for counterweight sets are grooved for the wire rope lift lines, and the Manila hand line. The head blocks are usually a larger diameter than the loft blocks.

C. Tension Pulley

The tension pulley (fig. 43), found on a single purchase counter-weight set, serves two functions.

43. Tension pulley

First, because it can "float," or move up and down, it can reduce strain on the hand line as increased humidity shrinks the rope. Some types of tension pulleys require a downward pressure on the front edge before they can move up on the bar guides.

The second function of the tension pulley is to allow the flyman to slacken the hand line in order to put a safety wrap on the hand line while loading or unloading. (See section 2.10.A.)

2.06   Lock Rail

The lock rail is a metal rail with a rope lock for the hand line of each counterweight set. The rope lock (fig. 44) is intended to keep the batten in a given position under a nearly balanced load condition. THE ROPE LOCK IS NEVER INTENDED TO HOLD A HEAVILY UNBALANCED LOAD while loading or unloading.

44. Rope lock

A. Lock

The lock consists of a pair of smooth jaws that are forced against the rope by a hand-operated lever arm. A steel ring that is threaded through the hand line slips over the lever when it is in the "UP," or locked, position. This ring locks the handle closed and keeps the handle from accidentally falling open (fig. 45).

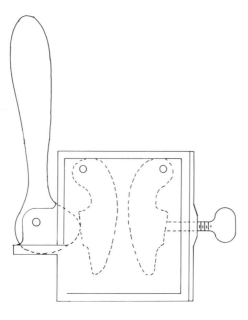

45. Rope lock detail

B. Lock Adjustment

The pressure of the jaws is designed to be easily adjusted by turning the thumbscrew on the back side of the lock. Missing thumbscrews should be replaced immediately.

C. Load Limit and Identification

The lock rail is a good place to mark the load limit of each rigging set, as well as identifying each set by number and use. Rigging sets are numbered from downstage to upstage.

2.07   Arbor

The arbor is the rack that holds the counterweights. It consists of a top and bottom plate, separated by two ¾" diameter steel rods. Steel plates called spreader plates or bars slide easily on the rods.

A top plate, with collars and thumbscrews, is called the "lock plate." As weights are stacked on the arbor, the spreader bars should be distributed every 3 to 4 feet. In the event that the counterweight set moves too fast and the arbor slams into the top or bottom stops, the spreader bars keep the rods from bending and the counterweights from falling out.

The lock plate should always be used on top of the counter-weights. Its function is to keep the counterweights from falling off the arbor. It can only do this if it is in place and the thumbscrews are tight (fig. 46).

46. Counterweights with spreader and lock plates in place

CAUTION: If the top and bottom arbor plates are cast iron, inspect them carefully and frequently for cracks.

A. Guide Systems

There are two types of guide systems for arbors. The simplest and noisiest is a wire guide system (fig. 47).

47. Wire guide counterweight set

Periodically, check the wires to see that they are tight and that they are not worn.

The second type is a track system, most commonly called a "T-bar" guide system. The name is derived from the shape of the guide rails (fig. 48).

48. T-bar guide counterweight set

The arbor has guide shoes, or rollers, that run on the rails. If the arbor becomes hard to move, check the guide and T-bars for proper alignment.

B. Pipe Weight

Most of the time, enough weight is left on the arbor to balance the batten weight. This is called the "pipe weight." It is good practice to paint these weights a distinctive color. This will aid the loaders when taking weights off the arbor.

NOTE: The spreader bars are *not* intended to mark pipe weight.

2.08　Hand Line

Most hand lines are Manila rope, although some experimentation is being done with various types of synthetic rope. If the rope becomes very tight or very slack, it should be adjusted by retying it.

On single purchase systems, this is done on the underside of the arbor (fig. 49).

49. Hand line tied at arbor bottom

The arbor is raised and locked off. The knot, usually two half hitches, is retied to adjust to the proper tension. Taping the tail of the rope to the hand line keeps it from getting in the way during operation.

On a double purchase set, one end of the hand line is tied off on the head block beam, and the other is tied off somewhere near the lock rail. Whichever knot is most convenient to reach may be used for adjustment. Since the knot is not moving, no taping is necessary. However, the end of the rope should be taped or whipped to prevent fraying.

2.09   Loading Bridge

The loading bridge is the platform where the arbors are loaded and unloaded. A safe loading bridge is placed at a height where the arbors can be easily reached when the battens are 3 to 4 feet above the stage floor. There should be adequate lighting so the loaders can safely see what they are doing.

A. Storing Weights

There should be a kick rail on both edges of the loading bridge to keep the counterweights from being kicked off (fig. 50). COUNTER-WEIGHTS SHOULD NEVER BE STACKED HIGHER THAN THE KICK RAIL!

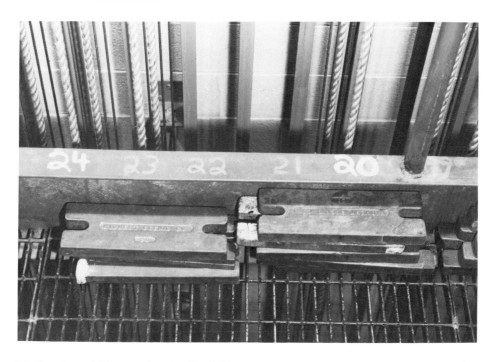

50. Counterweights stored on loading bridge

B. Loading and Unloading Weights

Usually two people should work on the loading bridge. One person hands the weights to the other, who loads them on the arbor. The transfer of weights is done over the loading bridge, never in the open space next to the arbor. The reverse is done for unloading. It is easiest for the person loading and unloading to grasp the weights in the middle (fig. 51).

51. Loading counterweights

The person handing the weights to the loader should hold them by the ends (fig. 52).

52. Handing weights to loader

C. Identifying Load Limits and Weights

It is good practice to post the weight of the various-sized counterweights in some obvious place on the loading bridge. The capacity of the batten can be indicated on the lock plate or other convenient locations.

2.10 Loading and Unloading Using a Loading Bridge

Counterweight sets are designed to be used in a balanced condition. This means that the load on the batten is equally balanced with the counterweights on the arbors. During the loading and unloading process, an *unbalanced* load condition exists. This condition is potentially VERY DANGEROUS! THE ENTIRE LOADING AND UNLOADING PROCEDURE SHOULD BE HANDLED WITH GREAT CARE. The basic rule for working with an unbalanced load is "KEEP THE WEIGHT DOWN." Never depend on the lock or the lock rail to hold weight in the air.

A. Crew Responsibilities

In order to avoid holding weight in the air, it is essential that a proper loading and unloading sequence be followed. In addition, it is essential that the crews loading weights, working the lock rail, and attaching scenery or lights to the battens thoroughly know their jobs.

1. The Flyman

The flyman on the lock rail directs the loading and unloading. He controls the sequence by giving directions for attaching or removing loads, as well as adding or removing counterweights. If a heavy show is being set in or taken out, assistant flymen operate the hand lines while the head flyman directs the operation. When loading or unloading, ALWAYS HAVE A SAFETY WRAP ON THE HAND LINE. There is always a chance of the counterweight set becoming unbalanced with the load in the air. Therefore, one of the methods of putting a safety wrap on the line should be used (figs. 53–57).

Method 1: Twist the Hand Line

53. Safety twist in hand line

60

Step down on the front of the tension pulley and pull up on the back hand line. This will create slack in the hand line. Twist one rope around the other, 4 or 5 times. Apply tension to one rope by hand, or place a belaying pin in the ropes for ease in holding. NEVER RELY ON THE ROPE LOCK TO HOLD AN UNBALANCED LOAD!

54. Belaying pin in hand line

55. Safety hitch on hand line

56. Line lok

Method 2: Tie a Safety Hitch from the Hand Line to the Lock Rail

Method 3: Use a Line Lok.

62

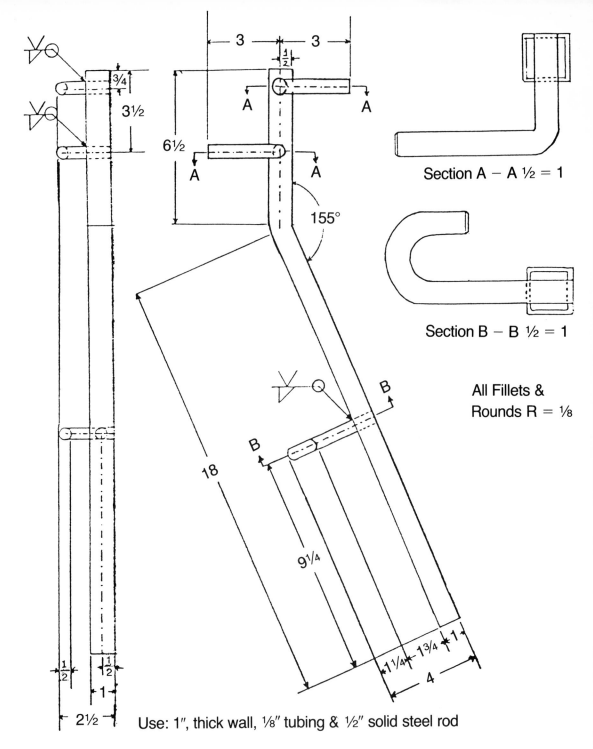

Section A − A ½ = 1

Section B − B ½ = 1

All Fillets &
Rounds R = ⅛

Use: 1″, thick wall, ⅛″ tubing & ½″ solid steel rod

57. Line lok detail. Courtesy Wes Jenkins

63

NOTE: I first saw a line lok in Calgary, Canada. Some months later, while doing a rigging seminar at the Banff Center, I mentioned the line lok. The technical director not only had some in the theatre but gave me the drawing (fig. 57) showing how to make one.

He mentioned that the device first appeared in Canada with a touring U.S. road show. This story is a typical example of how information on rigging is passed along from one place to another. NEVER LEAVE THE HAND LINE UNATTENDED WHEN A COUNTERWEIGHT SET IS BEING LOADED OR UNLOADED.

2. Loading Bridge Crew

The loading bridge crew should add or remove weights only when instructed to do so by the flyman. Adding weight to an arbor before a load is attached to a batten can cause an unbalanced condition. This could leave the counterweights hanging in the air, supported only by the hand line. Follow safe procedure for loading weights, using spreader bars and lock plates. (See section 2.08.)

3. Stage Crew

The crew onstage attaches the load to the batten. The head carpenter or head electrician supervises batten and spot line loading and unloading. The flyman gives the order to attach or remove the load to the stage crew. Removing the load from a batten before the arbor is unloaded is dangerous.

When scenery or curtains are resting on the floor while being attached or removed from a batten, their full weight is not offsetting the counterweights needed to balance them. The stage crew may have to hold the batten down as counterweights are being added or removed. They do this either by holding the batten with their hands or with a bull line. (See section 2.11.B.) WHEN HOLDING A BATTEN BY HAND, NEVER LEAN OVER THE BATTEN. IT MAY BE NECESSARY TO LET GO QUICKLY IF THE BATTEN BEGINS TO RUN AWAY.

B. Communications

The crews onstage, on the loading bridge, and at the lock rail must be able to hear the directions given by the flyman. If for any reason, the flyman has difficulty being heard, electronic voice reinforcement should be used.

There are often many people working on and above the stage. It is important to shout a warning to all before moving a batten in or out. The normal warning is to shout, "Heads up," or "Heads." It is also helpful to indicate where the piece is moving, i.e., "Upstage, heads up." WHEN WORKING ON THE STAGE, NEVER STAND OR WALK UNDER A MOVING RIGGING SET. NEVER MOVE A RIGGING SET WHEN SOMEONE IS UNDER IT.

C. Runaway Set

If anyone involved in loading or unloading a counterweight set loses his concentration, it is possible for him to make a mistake and for the set to become unbalanced and "run away." This happens when the weight in the air is so heavy that it cannot be held by the hand line. If it starts to creep, it may be possible to stop it by brute strength and quickly correct the situation. However, if the set begins to move rapidly, indicating a very heavy out-of-balance condition, DO NOT ATTEMPT TO STOP IT! To do so could cause serious injury. If a runaway should occur, follow this procedure:

1. Shout a warning to all crews.
2. Take cover. Everyone should take cover to protect themselves from flying counterweights and objects falling from the grid.

The arbor will either crash down or up, and the chance is great that counterweights, smashed head, or tension blocks, or other hardware will fly through the air. The batten will either go up or down, and the possibilities of it hitting adjacent flown objects, lift lines snapping, loft blocks smashing and falling, sprinkler systems being activated, are all very real. The only reasonable course of action is to get quickly out of harm's way. RUNAWAYS ARE CAUSED BY HUMAN ERROR. CONCENTRATION ON THE TASK AT HAND IS ESSENTIAL TO USING RIGGING SAFELY.

D. Loading

The loading procedure is as follows:

1. Attach load to batten. If a great deal of weight is resting on the floor, make provision for holding the batten down until the counterweight has been loaded.
2. Load counterweight arbor.
3. Slowly raise the batten to test for balance.
4. Add or subtract weight as needed for final balancing.

E. Unloading

1. Unload weight from arbor first.
2. Remove weight from batten.

2.11 Loading and Unloading without a Loading Bridge

Some facilities do not have loading bridges, or the arbors cannot be reached from the loading bridge when the batten is down. This is particularly true with lighting battens. The electric cable cradle often restricts the full travel of the battens and arbor.

A. Partial Loads

In the case where it is possible to attach partial loads to the batten, such as a lighting batten, the procedure is as follows:

1. Put a small amount of weight on the arbor—enough so that the flymen can safely raise the arbor to a height where the batten can be reached.

2. Add part of the load to the batten, overloading the batten slightly.

3. Lower the arbor so more weight can be added. This procedure is followed back and forth, until both batten and arbor are fully loaded and balanced. Needless to say, the flymen must be strong and in good physical condition for this work.

4. For unloading, the procedure is just reversed. Do not remove all of the load, or counterweights, at one time. This could result in a runaway set.

B. Unbalanced Large Loads

Sometimes it is necessary to attach large loads as a single unit. This requires moving either the arbor or batten with a great deal of weight in an unbalanced condition. While this is difficult, with proper techniques and planning the danger can be minimized. Sufficient force must be used to move the unbalanced load to a point where it can be balanced. Several options are possible.

1. Flymen Method

Weight permitting, a group of flymen operate the hand line by brute strength.

2. Bull Line

A bull line (fig. 58) can be used on the batten. A bull line is a long piece of hemp rope, ⅝″ to ¾″ diameter, that is doubled over the batten near one of the lift lines. The stage crew can then pull on this line and aid the flymen in raising or lowering an overweight arbor. The line is doubled so that it can be pulled free once the load is balanced. The bull line must be placed near a lift line or the batten can be bent. More than one bull line can be used on a batten.

58. Bull line on a batten

3. Capstan Winch

A capstan winch (fig. 59) is a movable winch that aids in pulling the arbor down, or holding the arbor from rising too rapidly. A rope is attached to the bottom of the arbor. It is then wrapped several times around the capstan of the winch and the winch is turned on. Applying tension to the free end of the rope causes it to tighten around the capstan and allows the winch to help move the unbalanced load.

59. Capstan winch. Courtesy Peter Albrecht Corporation

4. Block and Tackle

A block and tackle can be used to raise or lower an unbalanced load. It can be rigged to the head block beam and the top of the arbor to help lift an arbor-heavy load; or it can be rigged to the lock rail and the bottom of the arbor to help raise a batten-heavy load.

5. Sandbag Substitution

When battens are used to store scenery during a performance, there may not be time to unload the arbor when the scenery is removed from the batten. In order to keep the counterweight set in balance, a sandbag may be moved onstage on a dolly and attached to the batten near one of the lift lines. The weight of the sandbag will compensate for the weight of the removed scenery.

If the weight is heavy, the sandbag must be attached near one of the lift lines, or it will bow the batten. Remember, attach the sandbag *before* removing the scenery.

6. Carpet Hoist

The carpet hoist (fig. 60) is also used in situations where the load will be removed from the batten during performance. To make and use a carpet hoist, do the following:

   a. Bolt a bracket to the bottom of the arbor. The bracket should extend far enough to prevent the adjacent arbor from passing it. The bracket must be strong and rigid enough to move the scenery arbor without bending or breaking.

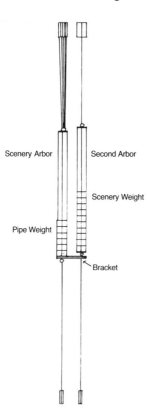

60. Carpet hoist

The bottom of the second arbor rests against the top of the bracket.
   b. The batten and lift lines must be removed from the second arbor.
   c. The scenery arbor is loaded only to pipe weight.
   d. The second arbor is loaded with enough weight to balance the scenery.
   e. To lower the scenery, pull the hand line on the scenery arbor. The weight on the second arbor will balance the load.

70

f. When the scenery is at the point where it will be removed from the batten, lock off the hand line on the second arbor. Secure a safety hitch to the second arbor hand line and lock rail. Remove the scenery from the batten. Take the batten out by using the hand line on the scenery arbor.

g. After the scenery is reattached to the batten, release the safety hitch and the rail lock on the second arbor. Raise the scenery by pulling on the second arbor hand line.

NOTE: When the scenery is removed from the batten, the second arbor is out of balance, and held in the air by the safety hitch. Be sure the hitch is well tied. NEVER DEPEND ON THE RAIL LOCK ALONE TO HOLD THE ARBOR!

2.12   Showtime Operation

The reason that scenery, curtains, or lights are flown is so that they can be used during a performance. Some flown objects do not move until the production is over. Others move in and out one or more times during a performance. It is essential to assure that the flown objects will function as they should for every performance.

A. Label Lock Rail

Each counterweight set in use for a production should be clearly labeled on the lock rail. Sets that are storing objects, not currently in use, should also be labeled. When releasing the lock on the lock rail, the flyman should know what is hanging on that batten.

B. Use Trim Marks

All rigging sets used during a performance should have trim marks on the hand lines. Tape, yarn, or string can be used for this purpose. If the piece must move quickly during the performance, winding the tape down the rope or inserting a warning yarn of a different color will indicate that the trim mark is approaching (fig. 61).

61. Tape trim mark

Pieces that do not move during a performance should also be marked, so that if they have to move for maintenance purposes, repositioning to performance trim is simplified.

C. Knuckle Buster

Accurate and fast positioning of a moving piece can be accomplished by using a knuckle buster on the hand line (fig. 62).

62. Knuckle buster

This clamp is designed to fit on the hand line, without damaging the rope lock. However, in the dim performance light, a flyman may hit his hand or knuckle on it—hence the name.

D. Preshow Testing

It is good practice to run each moving piece before every performance. Test for balance, clearance, and ease of running. If the pull on the hand line feels different, find out why—before the performance!

Because soft goods absorb moisture from the air, the weight of a curtain or drop can change drastically with a change in humidity. Adjusting the counterweight on the arbor may be necessary on a daily basis in some theatres.

E. Cueing

Be absolutely sure of the signals for all cues during a performance. A normal cue sequence consists of three parts, the first of which is a one-minute verbal warning. This will give the flyman time to find the proper hand line and determine what he is supposed to do. Does the piece move in or out? Are there special timing problems?

The next part of the cue is a "standby," which occurs about three lines before the "go" signal and is often done by turning on a cue light. At this point, the rope lock is released and the flyman is ready for the "go."

Finally, the "go" signal is given. Since it is impossible for the flyman to watch two things at one time, he generally watches the hand line to find the proper trim marks. The head flyman watches the moving piece to be sure that there are no clearance problems.

Should the flyman feel any unusual resistance, he should stop moving the piece immediately. Chances are that it is fouled on another batten or flown object. In this event, determine what the problem is before moving the piece. A powerful electric torch is a useful tool to have backstage for seeing into the dark flies.

2.13   Special Counterweight Rigging Problems

A. Light Battens

Light battens frequently change weight as they are raised or lowered. This is caused by the border light cable which is attached to the batten. In some rigging schemes, the cable is supported by a cradle attached to the lift lines. As the batten is raised, more weight is added to the batten. As the batten is lowered, weight is removed from the batten. In this circumstance, try to balance the batten for the performance trim height.

B. Variable Load

Flying framed wall units with hinged side panels is one situation in which a change in load on the batten occurs. As the wall unit touches the floor, and the hinged panels open, the floor—not the batten—is supporting the weight.

The wall tends to bounce off the floor, leaving a gap at the bottom of the set. Here are three suggestions for dealing with this problem.

1. Block and Tackle

Attach a block and tackle to the top of the arbor and the head block beam. (See section 2.11.B.) As the flown piece touches the floor, the block and tackle are used to raise the arbor and take the strain off the batten. This method requires the use of a second flyman. One flyman operates the hand line, the other operates the free end of the block and tackle.

2. Batten Tie-Down

Attach wire or hemp ropes to the batten near the lift lines. As the flown piece nears the floor, the free ends of the ropes are tied off to brackets firmly attached to the stage floor or to a sandbag. Using a trucker's hitch for hemp, or a lever-type load binder for a cable, will usually give the mechanical advantage needed to hold the batten in the desired position (figs. 63, 64).

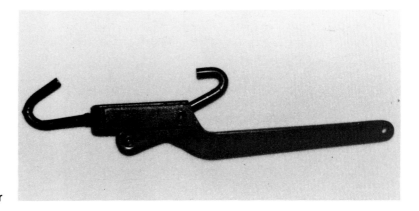

63. Load binder

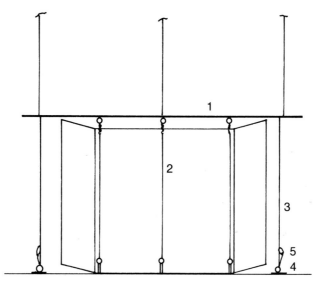

64. Batten tie-down

1 Batten
2 Attachment Line
3 Tie-Down Line
4 Ceiling Plate
5 Trucker's Hitch

3. Use a Carpet Hoist

See section 2.11.

75

C. Increasing Counterweight Capacity

There may be times when an arbor will not hold enough counter-weights to balance the heavy load. When this happens, suggested solutions include:

1. Join two or more adjacent battens together and use more than one arbor. When doing this, be sure that the load is firmly attached to all of the battens, and that the counterweight is evenly distributed among all the arbors. More than one flyman may be required to move the battens.

2. After a careful analysis of the components of the rigging set (i.e., cable size, loft block, head block strength, support steel) to be certain they can sustain the added weight, lead weights may be substituted for steel weights. The density of lead is approximately 1.45 times that of steel or cast iron.

3. Two adjacent arbors may be joined together. The lift lines can be removed from the second arbor and a clamping device to hold the arbors together can be devised.

4. An arbor extension may be built to hang under the arbor.

5. If there is room on the grid and in the flies, an additional free-hanging arbor may be used.

    a. Mount additional loft blocks over the batten. The blocks may be mounted evenly spaced between the permanently mounted loft blocks or near the point of attachment of a concentrated load.

    b. A head block or a group of loft blocks is mounted on the grid in an area where the arbor has clear travel.

    c. Attach lift lines from batten to arbor.

    d. Since the arbor may not be near a loading bridge, a safe method of loading the arbor will have to be devised.

    e. Arbor guide cables can be attached from grid to stage floor if necessary.

    f. The area under the arbor should be marked or roped off to keep people away during performance.

CAUTION: In items 2, 3, and 4 the flown object is solely sup-ported by *one* set of lift lines and blocks. IT IS ABSOLUTELY NECESSARY TO BE SURE THAT THE RIGGING SET AND SUPPORT STEEL CAN HOLD THE CONCENTRATED LOAD. Have a structural engineer make an analysis before attempting to increase the arbor load on any counterweight system.

2.14 Operation Summary

1. Safety inspect all components at regular intervals.
2. Know the feel, sound, and smell of the system.
3. Know the weight capacity of the system.
4. Always follow safe practice when loading, unloading, or operating the system. Keep unbalanced loads down.
5. Always have someone maintain visual contact with a moving piece.
6. Be sure the crew on the deck is clear of the piece before moving it.
7. Always warn people on the stage and grid before moving a batten during set in and strike.
8. Before each cue, check the cue sheet to be sure of which set to move, which direction, and any special timing problems.

2.15 Safety Inspection Summary

1. Hand lines.
2. Arbor: *a*) nuts on rods, *b*) spreader bars and lock plates, *c*) hand line knots, *d*) casting and weld cracks, *e*) guide system.
3. Head and loft blocks: *a*) mounting clamps, *b*) support steel, *c*) bearings.
4. Tension pulley: *a*) travel, *b*) bearings.
5. Lock rail: *a*) mounting bolts that hold the rail, *b*) rope lock mounting bolts, *c*) lock rings, *d*) lock adjustment.
6. Wire rope: *a*) weak and fraying, *b*) terminations at both ends.
7. Battens: *a*) splices, *b*) straightness.

Part 3   Motorized Rigging

3.01   Introduction

The basic hemp rigging used for the stage changed little from the time of the Greeks until the twentieth century. The need for greater efficiency prompted the modification of hemp to counterweight rigging around the beginning of the twentieth century. Counterweight rigging is still the most common type of rigging in use.

Today, motorized rigging is gaining acceptance in the theatre. Since the theatre industry has always been too small to support extensive primary research for its equipment, the development of various types of motors and controls has been paid for by other industries. Just as hemp rigging was borrowed from sailing ships, imaginative and creative theatre technicians have adapted motorized products for use in the theatre. A motorized system must be properly designed for its application by a competent engineer. Homemade systems and Rube Goldberg equipment can be extremely dangerous. DON'T USE IT.

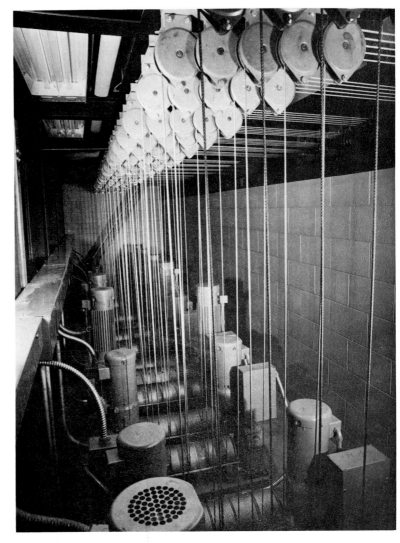

65. Electric motorized winches. Courtesy Peter Albrecht Corporation

66. Electric motorized winches. Courtesy Peter Albrecht Corporation

A number of theatrical rigging equipment manufacturers now offer motorized equipment as standard products (figs. 65, 66). Escalating labor costs and the versatility of motorized equipment have helped hasten its acceptance in theatre.

Some of the early motorized systems had design problems. They lacked consistency and dependability. As with any new technology, it took awhile to refine and debug the systems. Since the 1960s, much motorized rigging has been installed throughout the world. The better systems are extremely reliable, accurate, and dependable. Motorized systems are the "state of the art" in rigging equipment today.

It is beyond the scope of this book to describe all of the types of systems in existence. An attempt will be made to cover operating procedures for the most common types found in the United States.

The flyman operating motorized rigging does not have physical contact with the moving object, as he does with hemp and counterweight systems. THEREFORE, SPECIAL OPERATING PROCEDURES AND PRECAUTIONS FOR MOTORIZED RIGGING MUST BE FOLLOWED.

3.02 Systems Descriptions

The following descriptions are of general system types. Some of the advantages and problems are listed for each system.

A. Motorized Counterweight Systems

A motorized counterweight system is basically a counterweight set that uses a motor to do the pulling. The motors are usually quite small in horsepower, compared to a straight (noncounterweight) rigging system. Counterweights are still used to balance the load onstage, and the same basic loading and unloading procedures used for a counterweight set should be followed.

1. Chain Drive System

The chain drive system (fig. 67) uses a roller chain attached to the arbor, very much the same way that the hand line is attached to the arbor of a manual counterweight set. The chain goes from the top of the arbor over a head-block sprocket, down around a sprocket below the arbor, and finally attaches to the underside of the arbor.

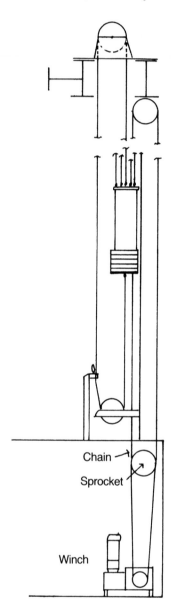

Chain

Sprocket

Winch

67. Chain drive
motorized
counterweight set

The winch is usually mounted on either the grid level or below the stage-floor level. To reduce motor noise and to save space, it is preferable to mount the motor in a separate machine room. Some systems use a drive cable in place of a roller chain. The basic operation principle is the same.

2. Traction Drive System

Traction drive systems (fig. 68) are generally used for constant weight systems, such as acoustical reflectors, speaker clusters, and movable ceiling panels. Once the arbor is loaded and the weight balanced, the weight is never changed. In this system, the head block is usually machined with tight V-shaped grooves for the lift lines. The head block is motorized and provides the force to move the load. As the motor turns the head block, the V grooves grip the cable and move the load. Special care should be taken to inspect the cable and traction head blocks for wear.

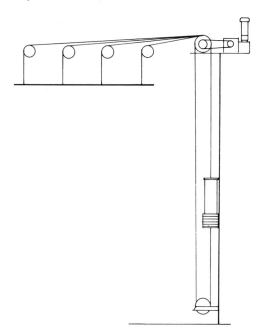

68. Traction drive motorized counterweight set

B. Straight Winch

The straight winch system uses only the winch to move and hold the load (fig. 69). This type of system usually requires a larger motor and gear reducer than a motorized counterweight system. But, it is very efficient on rigging sets with changing loads. Setup

83

and takedown are greatly sped up, because no counterweights need to be loaded or unloaded.

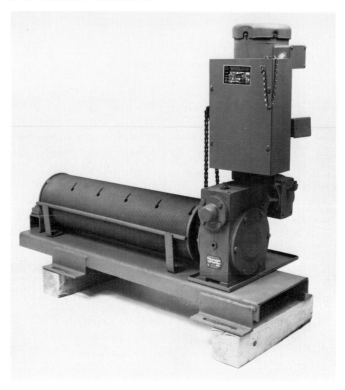

69. Constant speed electric winch. Courtesy Peter Albrecht Corporation

3.03   Motor Types

There are three types of motors that are generally used for motorized rigging. They each have characteristics that make them more useful for some applications than others.

A. AC Motor

An AC motor is the least expensive and easiest motor to operate for single speed applications.

B. DC Motor

This type of motor is reliable and dependable for variable speed applications. At the present time, it is also more expensive than an AC motor. Research being conducted currently may bring the price down in the near future.

C. Hydraulic Motor

A hydraulic system used for theatre work usually consists of the following components (fig. 70):

1. Hydraulic pump
2. Electric power supply
3. Hydraulic fluid feed line
4. Hydraulic fluid return line
5. Forward/reverse speed control manifold
6. Hydraulic motor
7. Forward fluid line
8. Reverse fluid line
9. Control wiring to manifold
10. Control panel
11. Control wiring to pump

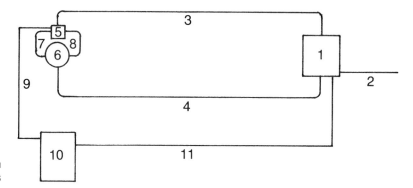

70. Hydraulic system components

A hydraulic motor by its nature is a variable speed motor. In this system, high-pressure hydraulic fluid is pumped through a motor which provides the lifting power. Hydraulic motor systems are very efficient, but require more maintenance than electric motors. Particular care should be given to filters, the fluid, valves, and hoses. To date, there are very few hydraulic systems in the United States.

3.04   Electric Winch Components

Electric winches usually consist of the following components (fig. 71). A) motor, B) gear reducer, C) brake, D) drum, E) controls, F) rigging components.

A. Motor

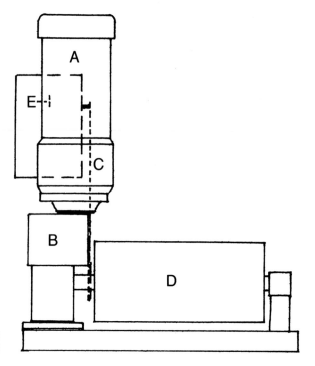

71. Electric winch
components

The motor is the device that converts electrical energy to mechanical energy. The motor is either AC or DC.

B. Gear Reducer

The gear reducer converts a high number of revolutions with low torque to a lower number of revolutions with a high torque (or lifting power). For many applications, self-locking gear reducers are preferred. These reducers require power to lower an object as well as raise it. The gear ratios are high enough so that the load cannot exert enough force to move the gears, even if no motor brake is attached to the system.

Nonself-locking, or overhauling, gear reducers work conversely. These reducers are often used where very high efficiency is required, or where the winches are self-climbing, such as in TV studios. In this case, when the brake is released on the system, the load is capable of turning the gears and descending without the motor running.

C. Brakes

Most electric winches use a motor brake. This brake is electrically held open when the winch is running. When the power is turned off, the brake closes and holds the load in place.

The brake must be properly sized for the application. The load should stop moving from full speed in 6″ or less.

Some winch systems employ a second brake system on the outboard end of the drum. This serves as a backup brake. If used with a self-locking gear reducer, the winch contains a triple brake system consisting of the motor brake, the drum brake, and the gear reducer.

D. Drum

On a straight electric winch, the lift lines wind up on a grooved drum. The drum is grooved for the size of the cable being used. A minimum of two dead wraps of cable should be maintained on the drum.

Nongrooved pile-on drums are sometimes used. These drums reduce the breaking strength of the cable, and must be used with great caution.

On multi-lined systems using pile-on drums, there is a tendency for the cables to wind unevenly.

E. Controls

Motorized rigging can be controlled in a number of different ways. Some of the typical components and methods are as follows:

1. Limit Switch

Most winches have a set of limit switches. These switches can be field adjusted for the maximum high and low trims. There should also be a set of overtravel switches which serves as backup for the limit switches. Should the limit switch fail, the overtravel switch will stop the movement of the winch before damage can occur.

2. Movement Controls

These controls can be categorized in two groups: hold-to-run and latching. The hold-to-run type requires constant hand pressure on the switch to keep the winch running. If pressure is removed, the winch stops. This type of control is the safest.

Latching-type controls require only that the control is activated to start the action. The control then is "latched" in, and the winch will run until a preset limit is reached. A separate control must be activated to stop the winch, in case of an emergency.

3. Emergency Stop Button

All motorized winch systems should have an emergency stop button. The button should be large, easy to see and reach, and require pressure to activate. This switch should not require electrical power to stop the machine.

Multi-winch systems will often have a single emergency stop button that will stop all machines.

4. Speed Controls

Variable speed systems will have a method of selecting and adjusting the speed of the winches. Some systems are designed to allow the synchronizing of several machines. While this may be a desirable function, it is very costly.

5. Position Control

Many systems will have some sort of device to allow for positioning. The important feature of positioning is repeatability. The load must stop at the same place when coming from the same direction every time. This feature is essential for the proper running of shows.

F. Rigging Components

The rigging components of motorized rigging (the loft blocks, cables, battens, etc.) are the same as those used in counterweight rigging. The same care and precautions should be used on these components of motorized equipment. (See part 2.)

3.05   Operation of Motorized Rigging

A single flyman can operate many motorized rigging sets simultaneously. This is both an advantage and a danger. Because the flyman does not have physical contact with the moving load through a hand line, it is imperative that visual contact with the moving load is maintained. If this is not possible, because of control location or because of the number of winches operating at one time, spotters—in audio contact with the winch operator—must be used.

It is absolutely necessary that the flyman knows the motorized equipment thoroughly. Answers to the following questions are essential before using any motorized system safely:

—What is the capacity of each winch?
—Are the gear reducers self-locking or overhauling?
—Are there overtravel switches on the limit switches?
—How do the controls work? (Hold-to-run? Latching?)
—How does the emergency stop switch work? (Disconnect the power to the entire system? Require power to activate?)

A. Safety Inspect all Components

As with any rigging system, motorized rigging sets must be periodically inspected. In addition to inspecting the normal rigging components (see part 2), check the following:

1. Be sure the correct size of fuse is installed.
2. Check all limit and overtravel switches.
3. Maintain oil in gear reducer or hydraulic systems according to manufacturer's instructions. Change the oil when necessary.
4. Test all controls for proper functioning.
5. Inspect winch mounting devices. They can pull loose!

B. System Capacity

It is essential to know the designed capacity of a motorized rigging set. Most are designed with the motor as the weakest part of the system. Any attempt to overload the system will result in the motor stalling out. However, not all systems are designed in this manner. Overloading the system can result in deflecting support steel or straining a component beyond its limit. FIND OUT THE CAPACITY OF THE SYSTEM, DISPLAY IT WHERE IT CAN BE SEEN, AND STAY WITHIN IT!

C. Loading and Unloading

1. Motorized Counterweight System

It is always best to run a motorized counterweight in a balanced condition. If it is severely overloaded, a great deal of strain is placed on the drive chain or cable. Listening to the motor run in both directions can be a good indication of whether the system is balanced or not. As with a straight counterweight system, keep the weight down when loading or unloading.

2. Straight Motorized System

Calculate the weight of the load before attaching it to the winch. If the machine stalls, blows a fuse, or sounds as if it is straining, it is overloaded. Do *not* use it in this condition.

D. Show Time Operation

When the equipment is in safe operating condition, the operator thoroughly understands the controls, and all loads have been correctly attached, the motorized equipment is ready to be used during performance.

If there are severe air currents backstage or tight clearance problems, do a preshow check of any pieces that might foul. Either maintain visual contact with moving pieces or use a spotter. Read the cue sheets carefully! Be sure the right piece is moving on cue.

Listen carefully for any unusual sounds. Stop the moving piece immediately if a strange noise is heard.

Most motorized systems will stop much faster than counterweight systems. This is a safety advantage in case of fouling.

3.06   Operation Summary

1. Safety inspect all components at regular intervals.
2. Know the system.
3. Know the weight capacity of each set.
4. Always follow safe practice when loading and unloading.
5. Be sure that everyone and everything are clear before moving a piece.
6. Maintain visual contact or use a spotter.
7. Always warn people onstage and on the grid before activating a winch during set-in or strike.
8. Before each cue, check your cue sheet to see which piece to move, which direction, and any special problems.

3.07   Safety Inspection Summary

1. All rigging components (see section 2.15).
2. All lubricated parts on the winches: *a*) gear box, *b*) pillow blocks, *c*) motor bearings.
3. Limit and overtravel switches.
4. Control system.
5. Emergency stop control.

Part 4 **Cutting and Knotting Rope, Attaching Loads, Special Problems**

4.01 Fiber Rope

Fiber rope is made of either natural or man-made fibers that are either twisted or braided into yarns and then into rope.

A. Cutting

There are specific procedures for cutting different kinds of rope.

1. Natural Fiber

Twisted natural fiber rope should be taped with electrician's friction tape before cutting. This tape is easy to remove and will keep the ends from fraying.

Tape about a 2″ length of rope where the cut is to be made. Use a pair of garden pruning shears and cut the rope in the center of the tape (fig. 72).

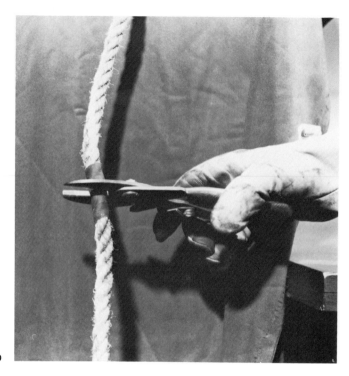

72. Cutting hemp

After the rope is cut, remove the tape and whip the end, using small twine (fig. 73).

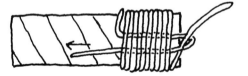

73. Whipping hemp

Braided natural fiber, such as cotton sash cord, need not be taped for cutting. Pruning shears work best for the job. If the rope is to be used for a long time, whipping, dipping the ends in glue, or taping will keep the ends neat. Braided rope is not as susceptible to fraying as twisted rope.

2. Synthetic Fiber

Synthetic fiber rope is best cut with a live flame. Hold the rope in both hands and rotate it over a flame. Gently pull it apart as you rotate it. The ends can be shaped before they completely cool by pushing them against a hard surface. This method not only cuts the rope but binds the fiber ends together to prevent unraveling (fig. 74).

74. "Cutting" nylon rope

B. Knots

A knot is used to attach a rope to an object. Knots reduce the breaking strength of rope and can slip or come untied if misapplied. Therefore, the proper knot for a specific application must be used.

1. Bowline

Use this knot (fig. 75) when tying a loop in the end of a rope.

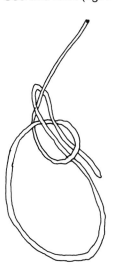

75. Bowline

2. *Clove Hitch*

This knot is used for tying a rope to a rigid object, such as a batten. When properly tied, it does not slip sideways.

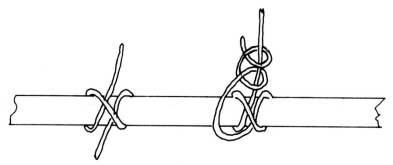

76. Clove hitch with a half hitch

3. *Rolling Hitch*

This knot (fig. 77) is used to tie the safety rope on a counterweight handline. (See section 2.10.A-1.)

77. Rolling hitch

4. Half Hitch

The half hitch (fig. 78) can be used to secure the counterweight safety rope to the lock rail.

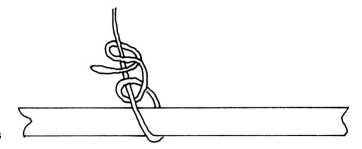

78. Two half hitches

25. Figure-8 Knot

The figure-8 (fig. 79) knot is used at the end of a spot line to hold a length of pipe as a weight. (See section 1.07.)

79. Figure-8 knot

6. Trucker's Hitch

This knot (fig. 80) is used when flying framed scenery with hemp, or tying a batten down to a floor hold. (See section 2.13.B.).

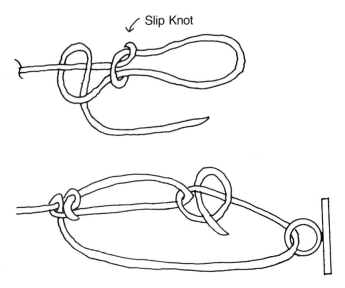

Slip Knot

80. Trucker's hitch

4.02   Wire Rope

Cutting, handling, and terminating wire rope all require special care. Carelessness can result in damage and loss of strength to the rope.

A. Cutting

There are several different kinds of wire rope cutters available on the market. For sizes up through ⅛", small hand-held cutters can be used (fig. 81).

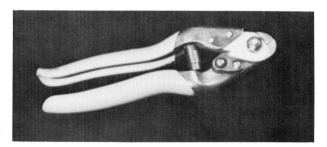

81. Small wire rope cutter

For larger sizes, two hand cutters or a cold chisel must be used (fig. 82).

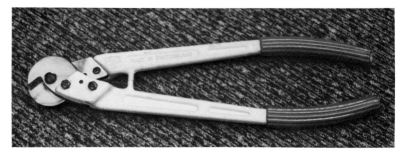

82. Large wire rope cutter

NEVER try to use a standard pair of wire cutters! Not only will they do a poor job, but they will be ruined in the process.

Tape the cable before cutting. If the cable is to have a free end, "seizing" is required. Seizing is whipping the end with thin wire (fig. 83).

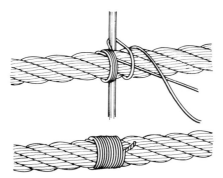

83. Seizing wire rope. Courtesy American Iron and Steel Institute, *Wire Rope Users Manual*

B. Unreeling and Uncoiling

Great care should be taken when unreeling or uncoiling cable. Carelessness can cause kinking. A kink can never be removed and must be cut out of the cable.

When taking cable from a reel, place the reel on an axle so that it can rotate. Grasp the cable and walk away from the reel. Take care that the reel does not turn too fast and dump cable in a pile on the ground.

If the reel is too large to be supported by an axle, let the end of the cable rest on the floor, and roll the reel away from the end.

Coiled lengths of wire rope must be handled very carefully. Unroll the coil in your hand as you walk along, or roll it along the floor. DO NOT UNCOIL BY PULLING ONE END.

C. Terminating

Terminating (attaching the end of wire rope to an object) must be done carefully. It is important to maintain maximum cable strength. It is also necessary to be sure that the termination will not slip.

A thimble is always used when forming a loop in the end of a wire rope. The rope is fastened using either cable clips or nicopress sleeves.

1. Cable Clips*

Cable clips come in two types, U-bolt and fist grip. The efficiency of both types is the same.

When using U-bolt clips, extreme care must be exercised to make certain that they are attached correctly, i.e., the U-bolt must be applied so that the U section is in contact with the dead end of the rope. Also, the tightening and retightening of the nuts must be accomplished as required.

[Various codes and regulatory agencies require a minimum of three clips on all sizes of wire rope. To this author's knowledge, there is no information available that the addition of an extra clip increases the breaking strength of the wire rope above 80%. REMEMBER, NEVER SADDLE A DEAD HORSE.—J. O. G.]

U-BOLT

Clip Size	Min. No. of Clips	Amount of Rope to Turn Back	Torque in Lbs./Ft.
⅛	2	3¼	4.5
³⁄₁₆	2	3¾	7.5
¼	2	4¾	15
⁵⁄₁₆	2	5¼	30
⅜	2	6½	45
⁷⁄₁₆	2	7	65
½	3	11½	65

From the Crosby Group

*Information in section 4.02.C-1 is from the *Wire Rope Users Manual,* 2d ed., Copyright © 1981 by American Iron and Steel Institute, and is reprinted with permission of the American Iron and Steel Institute.

84. U-bolt wire rope clip. Courtesy American Iron and Steel Institute, *Wire Rope Users Manual*

Right Way for Maximum Rope Strength

Wrong Way: Clips Staggered

85. Clip application. Courtesy American Iron and Steel Institute, *Wire Rope Users Manual*

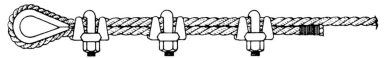

Wrong Way: Clips Reversed

Recommended method of applying U-bolt clips to get maximum holding power of the clip (figs. 84, 85):

1. Turn back the specified amount of rope from the thimble. Apply the first clip one base width from the dead end of the wire rope (U-bolt over dead end—live end rests in clip saddle). Tighten nuts evenly to recommended torque.

2. Apply the next clip as near the loop as possible. Turn on nuts firm but do not tighten.

3. Space additional clips, if required, equally between the first two. Turn on nuts—take up rope slack—tighten all nuts evenly on all clips to recommended torque.

4. NOTICE! Apply the initial load and retighten nuts to the recommended torque. Rope will stretch and be reduced in diameter when loads are applied. Inspect periodically and retighten to recommended torque.

A termination made in accordance with the above instructions, and using the number of clips shown, has an approximate 80% efficiency rating. This rating is based on the nominal strength of wire rope. If a pulley is used in place of a thimble for turning back the rope, add one additional clip.

The number of clips shown is based on using right regular or lang lay wire rope, 6 × 19 class or 6 × 37 class, fiber core or IWRC, IPS or EIP. If Seale construction or similar large outer wire-type construction in the 6 × 19 class is to be used for sizes 1″ and larger, add one additional clip.

The number of clips shown also applies to right regular lay wire rope, 8 × 19 class, fiber core, IPS, sizes 1½″ and smaller and right regular lay wire rope, 18 × 7 class, fiber core, IPS or EIP, sizes 1¾″ and smaller.

For other classes of wire rope not mentioned above, it may be necessary to add additional clips to the number shown.

If a greater number of clips are used than shown in the table, the amount of rope turnback should be increased proportionately. ABOVE BASED ON USE OF CLIPS ON NEW ROPE.

FIST GRIP CLIP

Clip Size	Min. No. of Clips	Amount of Rope to Turn Back	Torque in Lbs./Ft.
³⁄₁₆–¼	2	4	30
⁵⁄₁₆	2	5	30
⅜	2	5½	45
⁷⁄₁₆	2	6½	65
½	3	11	65

From The Crosby Group

How to Apply Fist Grip Clips

86. Fist grip clips. Courtesy American Iron and Steel Institute, *Wire Rope Users Manual*

Recommended method of applying fist grip clips (fig. 86):

1. Turn back the specified amount of rope from the thimble. Apply the first clip one base width from the dead end of the wire rope. Tighten nuts evenly to recommended torque.

2. Apply the next clip as near the loop as possible. Turn on nuts firmly but do not tighten.

3. Space additional clips if required equally between the first two. Turn on nuts—take up rope slack—tighten all nuts evenly on all clips to recommended torque.

4. NOTICE! Apply the initial load and retighten nuts to the recommended torque. Rope will stretch and be reduced in diameter when loads are applied. Inspect periodically and retighten to recommended torque.

A termination made in accordance with the above instructions, and using the number of clips shown, has an approximately 80% efficiency rating. This rating is based on the catalogue breaking strength of wire rope. If a pulley is used in place of a thimble for turning back the rope, add one additional clip.

The number of clips shown is based on using right regular or lang lay wire rope, 6 × 19 class or 6 × 37 class, fiber core or IWRC, IPS or EIPS. If Seale construction or similar large outer wire-type construction in the 6 × 19 class is to be used for sizes 1″ and larger, add one additional clip.

The number of clips shown also applies to right regular lay wire rope, 8 × 19 class, fiber core, IPS, sizes 1½″ and smaller; and right regular lay wire rope, 18 × 7 class, fiber core, IPS or EIPS, sizes 1½″ and smaller.

For other classes of wire rope not mentioned above, it may be necessary to add additional clips to the number shown.

If a greater number of clips are used than shown in the table, the amount of rope turnback should be increased proportionately. ABOVE BASED ON USE OF FIST GRIP CLIPS ON NEW WIRE ROPE.

IMPORTANT: Failure to make a termination in accordance with aforementioned instructions, or failure to periodically check and retighten to the recommended torque, will cause a reduction in efficiency rating.

Fist grip clips do not damage the cable the way U-bolt clips do. For this reason, they are preferred for temporary uses, such as hanging scenery.

2. Nicopress Sleeves

When properly applied, copper nicopress sleeves (fig. 87) will provide a termination with 100% efficiency. Carefully follow the manufacturer's instructions.

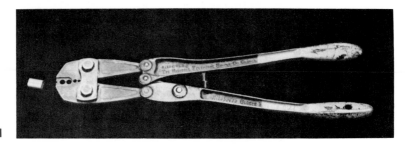

87. Nicopress tool

Figures 88 through 91 illustrate the proper way to apply a sleeve to ³⁄₁₆ aircraft cable.

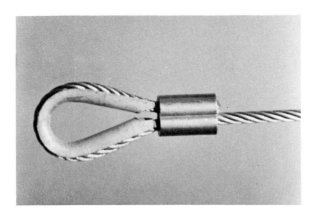

88. Nicopress sleeve on ³⁄₁₆ aircraft cable

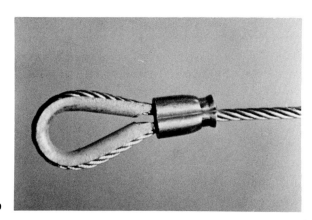

89. First crimp

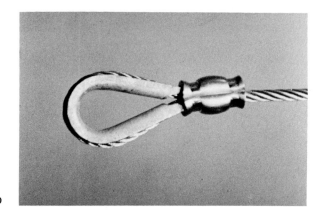

90. Second crimp

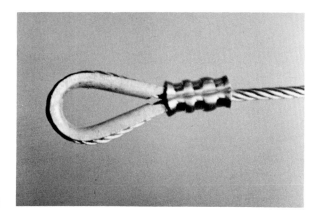

91. Third crimp

a. Align the sleeve with about ⅛" of cable protruding from the top of the sleeve.

b. Make the top crimp.

c. Make the bottom crimp.

d. Make the middle crimp.

e. Check the crimps with manufacturer's go/no-go gauge (fig. 92). If necessary, adjust tool and crimp again. The tool should be checked after every fifty crimps.

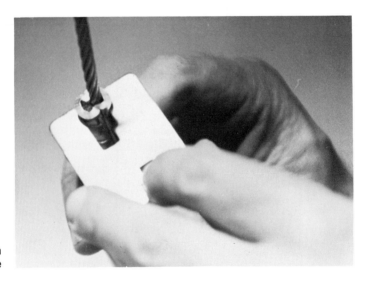

92. Checking with go/no-go gauge

3. Trim Chains

Trim chains can be used to attach wire rope to battens as discussed in section 2.04.C. They can also be used in many ways to attach loads to battens. A typical scenery trim chain consists of a welded or forged steel ring, a length of chain, and a device to attach the chain to itself (usually a snap hook). One should take care to find out the safe working load of a trim chain before using it.

Consulting manufacturers' catalogues will usually give that information on the chain and the ring. It is almost impossible to find a rating for snap hooks. The chain can either be attached to the batten by sliding the ring on the batten between the lift lines, passing the chain around the batten and through the ring, or wrapping the chain around the batten one and one-half times and attaching it to itself (fig. 93).

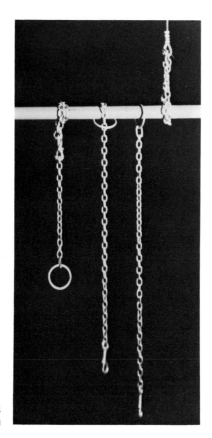

93. Trim chains on a
batten

If the strength of the trim chain is in doubt, don't use it, or use more chain to distribute the load. If the strength of the snap hook is in doubt, use a bolt or shackle.

4.03   Attaching Loads

A. Curtains

Curtains are attached to battens using tie lines. Some of the standard procedures for tying curtains are as follows:

1. Knots

Always use bow knots. This knot will securely hold the load and untying the curtain will be easy.

105

2. Full Stage-Width Curtains

On full stage-width curtains, start tying in the center of the batten.

3. Excess Curtain Width

Fold excess curtain back on the offstage side.

4. Overlap Panels

Overlap panels by at least one tie line. Overlapping by two will ensure a less obvious break in the panels.

5. Tied-in Fullness

When tying fullness into a flat-sewn curtain, tie the ends first (fig. 94). Then tie the center tie to a center point on the batten between the two end ties. Continue tying the center tie of the remaining section of curtain to the center of the remaining spaces. This will produce even fullness in the goods.

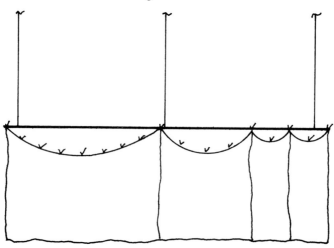

94. Tying fullness into a curtain

6. Soft Edge Legs

For a softer look on the onstage edge of legs, fold the sewn edge back one or more ties.

7. Bent Batten

If the legs on the batten are very heavy and bend the batten, apply weight to the center of the batten. Use either sandbags or a length of pipe tied, chained, or clamped to the batten.

B. Drops

Drops are either made with grommets and ties or sandwich battens.

1. Grommets and Ties

Tie a drop to a batten the same way that a full stage-width curtain is tied. Start at the center point and work toward the offstage ends.

2. Sandwich Batten

The top of a drop can be sandwiched between two pieces of 1″ × 3″ pine that are screwed together. The drop is pierced just below the sandwich batten near the ends, and about every 10 feet. Trim chains can then be used to attach the drop to the pipe batten (fig. 95).

95. Scenery trim chains

The chains are attached to the pipe batten by passing the free end around the batten and through the ring. The chains are pulled snug to the pipe batten. The free end is then passed through the drop and snapped back on the chain. This method allows easy leveling of crooked drops.

An alternate method is to drill ½″ holes through the sandwich batten and use no. 8 sash cord to tie the drop to the pipe batten.

3. Pipe Weight

A common method of weighting a drop is to sew a pocket into the bottom and insert a length of ½″ pipe as a weight. Be sure the ends of the pipe are secured to the drop to prevent the pipe from slipping out if one end of the drop should foul.

4. Pipe Weight Safety

Use safety cables if the drop requires a pipe larger than ½", or if it is so close to another object that there is danger of the pipe pocket tearing and the pipe falling out.

Attach ¹⁄₁₆" or ⅛" wire rope to the pipe batten every 10 or 12 feet and near the ends of the drop. Let the cables hang down on the back side of the drop. Pierce the pipe pocket on the back side, then secure the other end of the cables to the batten weight pipe, using a clove hitch and cable clip. Even if the drop tears completely away, the safety cables will hold the weight pipe. SAFETY CABLES ARE A MUST FOR ALL DROPS USED IN "A-VISTA" CHANGES. ¹⁄₁₆" cable will usually be strong enough and, if painted black, will not be noticeable even through a scrim.

C. Vertical Framed Scenery

Vertical framed scenery is anything that has a rigid frame and hangs in a vertical plane.

1. Hardware Attachment

Put at least one bolt through every piece of hardware on a flying unit. This is especially important on all hanger irons used to attach the unit to fly lines.

2. Calculate Load

The load will probably not be evenly distributed to all support lines (see fig. 13). Be sure the support lines have a ratio of a 5 to 1 safety factor. If people must move under the load while it is moving, increase the safety factor to 10 to 1.

3. Hardware

The weight of a framed piece should always be held by the *bottom member* of the frame. Top hanger irons are guides for the supporting rope or cable. All hardware should be bolted to the scenery.

4. Attaching with Rope

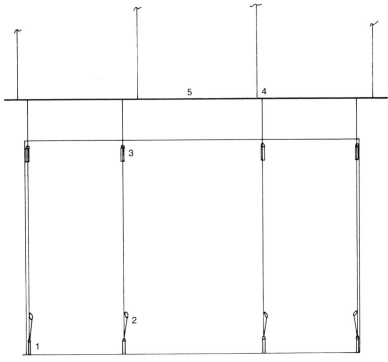

1 Bottom Hanger Iron
2 Trucker's Hitch
3 Top Hanger Iron
4 Clove Hitch
5 Batten

96. Framed scenery
hung with rope

Rope is used when the weight of the unit is within the load limits of rope and when the attaching lines will not be visible (fig. 96). Tie the rope to the batten with a clove hitch and two half hitches. Pass the rope through the top hanger irons (fig. 97).

97. Top hanger iron

Attach it to the bottom hanger irons using a trucker's hitch (fig. 98).

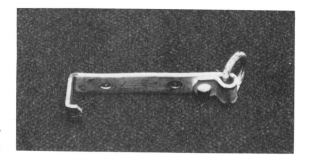

98. Bottom hanger iron

The hitch will allow easy adjustment for leveling the unit.

5. Attaching with Wire Rope

Attach the cable to the batten by wrapping it around the batten with a clove hitch and fastening the end with cable clips. An alternate method is to make a loop around a thimble, using cable clips or nico-press sleeves. This loop is then attached to a trim chain on the batten.

99. Boat eye

The cable is then run through a boat eye (fig. 99) and attached to a jaw/eye turnbuckle.

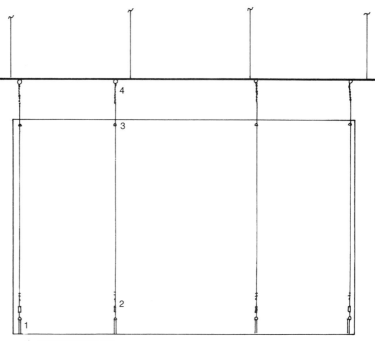

1 Bottom Hanger Iron
2 Turnbuckle
3 Boat Eye
4 Trim Chain

100. Framed scenery
hung with wire rope

The jaw end is attached to the bottom hanger iron. Leveling of the piece can then be easily accomplished from the bottom (fig. 100).

D. Horizontal Framed Scenery

Horizontal framed scenery units (fig. 101), such as ceilings, hang parallel to the stage floor. It is important to have enough pickup points to distribute the load on the frame. Ceiling plates (fig. 102) bolted to the frame, are used to attach pickup lines of either hemp or wire rope.

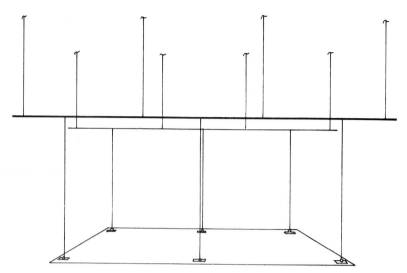

101. Horizontal
framed scenery

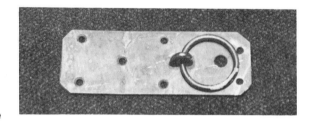

102. Ceiling plate

E. Point Loads

A point load is the load on a single support point (fig. 103).

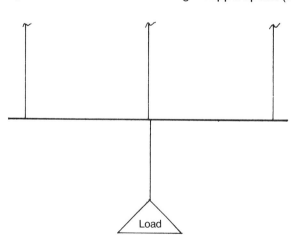

103. Point load on a
batten

Load

The point must be capable of supporting the load imposed on it. When attaching a load to a batten, it is best to keep the attachment points as close to the lift lines as possible. This will keep the batten from bending and lift line cables from becoming slack (fig. 104).

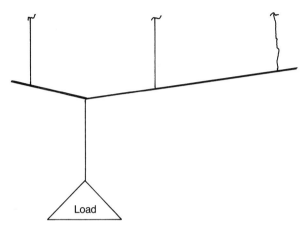

104. Point load bending batten

1. Truss Batten

One method of distributing the load more evenly is to use a truss batten (fig. 105). The truss is made of two battens (spaced from several inches to a foot apart) with welded or bolted support members.

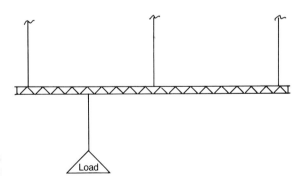

105. Point load on a truss batten

2. Bridling

Bridling is another way to distribute the load (fig. 106).

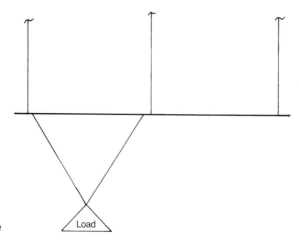

106. Load on a bridle

    The same technique can be used to distribute dead-hung loads attached to the grid.

    NOTE: The strength of the bridling lines is reduced as the angle of the lines increases (fig. 107).

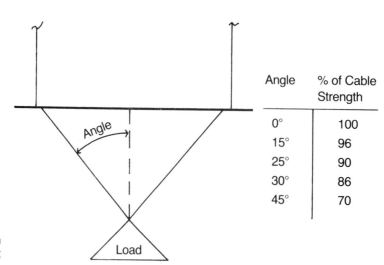

107. Bridle strength reduction chart

Angle	% of Cable Strength
0°	100
15°	96
25°	90
30°	86
45°	70

When using a bridle for a single point load, use a welded ring to attach the three lines (fig. 108).

108. Bridle line detail

4.04 Special Problems

A. Breasting

There are times when it is necessary to move a flown piece in a horizontal, as well as a vertical, direction. This can be done by breasting the piece (fig. 109).

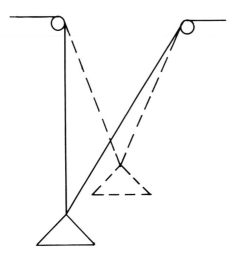

109. Breasting

B. Tripping

Tripping is a method of flying a very high drop where the grid is too low (fig. 110). A second set of lift lines is attached to the weight pipe in the bottom of the drop.

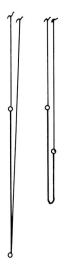

110. Tripping

   As the trip lines are raised, the load on the main flying set is reduced. The hand line of the main flying set should be tied off with a safety hitch before raising the trip lines.

C. Guiding

In very close quarters, a drop or piece of scenery may require guide cables to keep from fouling (fig. 111).

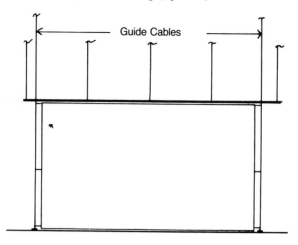

111. Guide lines on a drop

If guide cables are not possible, lengths of rope, called tailing ropes, can be attached to the end of the batten or an adjacent batten (fig. 112). As the piece is moving in or out, crew members guide it with the tailing ropes.

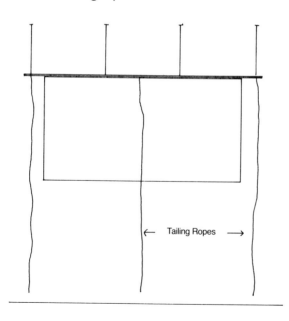

112. Tailing ropes on a batten

D. Dead Hanging

Units may be dead hung from the grid. When necessary, distribute the load to more than one grid member (fig. 113). If bridling is not possible, pass the support line through the grid and attach it to a piece of steel or wood that has been laid on the grid. This will help to distribute the load.

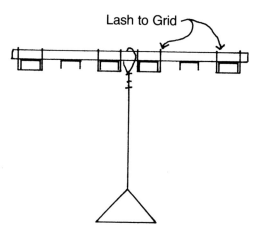

Lash to Grid

113. Distributing a dead hung load on the grid

Appendix

Recommended Guidelines for Stage Rigging and Stage Machinery

Specifications and Practices as
Developed by the
United States Institute
for Theatre Technology

Edited by PAUL J. BRADY and JAY O. GLERUM

Reprinted with permission of the United States Institute for Theatre Technology.

1   Operation and Maintenance

Equipment

Technical stage equipment shall be manufactured, installed, operated, and maintained in such a way that its safety and function are assured.

Technical stage equipment shall be inspected before the initial use, after any alterations to the operation or design of system, and at regular intervals. These inspections shall be conducted by experts in technical stage equipment.

Operation, maintenance, and repair work on technical stage equipment shall be done only by those persons having proper training and qualifications.

If technical stage equipment is found to have defects which may result in personal injury or property damage, the equipment shall be declared unsafe, and rendered inoperative, until such time as the defect(s) have been corrected. Defect(s) in engineering or manufacturing shall be reported to the manufacturer who, in turn, will take corrective action.

Persons charged with the operation of technical stage equipment shall be thoroughly instructed in the following:

The operation and functioning of the equipment

The safe recommended use of the equipment

The necessary routine maintenance work for safe operation

The operation of all safety devices

Possible dangers during normal operations as well as the increased danger potential during improper operation

Procedures during accidents and malfunctions

Upon completion of a training session persons charged with the operation of technical stage equipment shall sign a statement indicating that they have received instruction in the safe operation of the specific system.

Where suspended scenery components are moved by guided hand-pulled ropes or wire ropes, the weight of the components shall not exceed a balanced load by more than 40 lbs. Should this not be the case, the scenery component shall be balanced with a counterweight to bring the imbalance to less than 40 lbs. Exceptions to this rule may be taken only during load-in and strike of scenery when proper precautions are taken.

Buffering or shock-absorbing devices, which reduce hard contact between the counterweight carriage and the upper and the lower stops, shall be installed.

Hard contact is a sudden (or uncontrolled) contact with the upper or lower limits of the travel of the counterweight carriage.

The installed counterweights shall be secured against falling from the counterweight carriage during operation.

The operating gallery and catwalks shall be equipped with safety railings and toe boards.

The loading gallery/platform shall have a sign stating counterweight storage limit in lbs. per sq. ft. and not to exceed the height of the toe board.

Counterweight stored on the deck of the gallery/platform shall not exceed 75% of the total deck area. The area of the deck immediately in front of the counterweight carriages shall be kept clear at all times.

Motorized counterweight systems shall have suitable safeguards to prevent persons from accidentally reaching or walking into the path of the moving counterweight carriages.

Spreader plates, top spacers, hold-down plates, etc., shall be manufactured in such a way as to be safely secured until needed. Spreader plates shall be employed at all times. Each counterweight carriage shall have enough spreader plates to allow for one plate for every 2 lineal feet of applied counterweight.

Counterweight carriages shall be marked in such a way as to indicate the appropriate locations of spacer plates during the loading process.

The floor of the loading gallery or catwalk, and the bottom of the counterweight carriage at maximum high trim, shall allow for safe access at all times to the entire counterweight carriage.

The flying system design and installation shall provide some mechanism, other than the rope lock, to prevent counterweight carriage travel during the loading and unloading operations.

Manual rigging systems without a loading floor shall be provided with a capstan winch capable of raising or lowering a fully loaded out-of-balance counterweight carriage.

Trim chains shall have a safety factor of 8 to 1 and shall be attached to the lifting line or wire rope with use of appropriately sized thimbles and wire rope clamps or thimbles and nicopress sleeves. For temporary attachment to a batten one and one-half wraps around are minimum with the chain attached to itself with load-rated hardware.

Suspended Work Areas

Gridiron, catwalks, and loading galleries shall be accessed only by personnel directly engaged in work in these areas.

Prior to engaging in overhead work all line sets shall be secured and all areas below shall be secured or posted to prevent unauthorized entry.

No objects may be stored or temporarily placed on the gridiron. Proper containers shall be provided for those items used during maintenance, setup, and strike. All tools shall be tethered to either the structure or the user.

2   Marking and Labeling

Manufacturer

A manufacturer's label shall be conspicuously and permanently attached to each piece of technical stage equipment.

Visible and permanent system capacity information shall be displayed at a location that is easily seen by the operator.

The capacity of the gridiron, catwalks, and galleries in lbs. per sq. ft. shall be conspicuously displayed.

Master switches, emergency switches, and emergency keys (or other devices with similar purpose) shall be identified and marked with the O.S.H.A. "Red T" color.

Those parts of technical stage equipment that require lubrication and maintenance shall be safely and easily accessible and serviceable. The name and type of the lubricant shall be conspicuously displayed near the lubrication points. Lubrication points shall be conspicuously marked.

Operation

Critical instructions for a given piece or similar group of technical stage equipment shall be visibly mounted at the operating and/or control station. Such instructions shall be brief and concise, e.g., "cut in case of fire," "disable when not in use," etc.

3   Safety and Protective Measures

Hoisting equipment shall be secured against unauthorized and inadvertent use.

For the suspension of flying equipment, wire ropes with a minimum safety factor of not less than 8 must be used.

Contact Protection

Rotating and moving parts shall be covered and/or protected so that persons cannot be injured. Equipment located in normally inaccessible rooms or areas shall be considered properly protected.

Speed Limits

The speed of moving equipment shall be adapted to the operating conditions.

When moving stage equipment is used, the operator shall have constant visual contact with the moving piece. If this is not possible a spotter or visual monitoring device shall be required.

Lift Limit

Powered pulling, lowering, and lifting devices shall have limit switches for the lowest and highest positions.

Emergency Switch

A power disconnect switch shall be located within reach of the operator.

All rigging equipment shall be labeled in accordance with section 3 of this Appendix.

Lighting bridges and work gangways that are not permanently connected to the structure of the building shall be equipped to assure safe access.

4   Requirements for System Elements in Lifting Applications

Individual counterweight used in working line sets shall not exceed 40 lbs.

Weights installed to offset heavy permanent loads on electrics, light bridges, house curtains, and the like, shall be sized as required.

Deflecting devices or catch grids are recommended where counterweight systems are positioned above working areas.

All components utilized in stage rigging equipment shall be specifically recommended by their manufacturer or trade organization for hoisting applications. They shall be installed and used in accordance with the manufacturer's specifications.

Rigging system components shall be mounted with fasteners designed to prevent accidental loosening and detachment.

Drives

Positive locking connecting devices between the drive and the driving pulley, the wire rope drum, the shaft, the sprocket wheel, etc., are permitted without restriction.

Only positive connecting devices that connect the drive with the driven shall be allowed. The drive and the driven may be disconnected for servicing only after the load has been secured against any movement.

Before and during any servicing that requires the drive to be disconnected from the driven, all attached loads shall be safely restrained from movement.

In technical stage equipment with hydraulic drive, an impermissible pressure increase shall be safely prevented.

Hydraulic and electromechanical power systems shall have adjustable limit stops provided for the final operating positions.

Hydraulically and electromechanically driven equipment shall have acceleration/deceleration ramps which prevent sudden inertial changes to any attached items. These ramps shall function at all times and in all positions. Excepted is an emergency situation when the emergency stop switch is activated.

When the direction of travel is to be changed in hydraulically driven equipment, the movement of the device is to come to a controlled stop before the change can be executed.

Hoses for hydraulic devices shall be certified by the manufacturer for the maximum design pressure for the given application.

High-pressure tubing and piping shall be correctly and rigidly secured to the structure in order that whipping is prevented should a rupture occur. In temporary and permanent installations, care shall be taken to secure the devices to the floor, the building structure, and the equipment frame.

In the event of a rupture, a device shall be included which disables the system or that portion of the system affected by the rupture.

There shall be engineering data that assure that, in case of failure or a malfunction of the hydraulic equipment, movement is controlled.

In technical stage equipment with optional manual or power drive, selection shall be mutually exclusive, so that one is switched off while the other drive is in use.

Manually operated technical stage equipment shall be designed in such a way that the force used by the operator does not exceed 50 lbs.

In drive elements that transmit torque for vertical load movements, press fits alone are not permitted.

Lowering of loads with power-driven hoisting units must occur with a switched-on motor. Excepted are protective curtains and hydraulically driven hoisting units.

Brakes and Locking Devices

Manually operated winches shall be equipped with an effective locking device against return motion and with a self-locking brake. This equipment is not necessary if self-locking gears are used.

The brakes of the manually operated winches shall be designed as load-pressure brakes. If the winches are equipped with ratchet handles, the movement of the ratchet handle may not exceed 60° total travel, or plus/minus 30° from center.

Winches with hand cranks designed to hold suspended loads shall have a brake that is normally on. The locking element used for this purpose must create a positive lock with the drum.

Power-driven hoisting units for technical stage equipment shall be equipped with spring-loaded electrically or hydraulically released brakes capable of stopping the rated load within a reasonable distance.

Electrically driven wire rope elevators of technical stage equipment intended for regular conveyance of persons shall be equipped with two mutually independent brakes. One of the brakes is to be installed in such a way that its effectiveness is not impaired by drive damage. Each brake shall be individually testable. If a counterweight is present, and the maximum live load is less than 20% of the lifting floor or car, only one brake is required. In self-locking hoist drives, only that brake remaining effective in case of drive damage is required.

Horizontal pulling devices not driven via worm gears shall have one brake.

Horizontal pulling devices driven via worm gears with a 40 to 1 or greater ratio do not require a brake.

Wire Rope Drum

Motor-driven drums shall be manufactured so that the wire rope is wound in single layer only. All metal drums shall have machined grooves as specified in the current edition of the *Machinery Handbook.*

Excepted are those drums that allow the wire rope to stack only on its own width.

Motor-driven winches shall be manufactured so as to prevent the wire rope from leaving the ends of the drum.

Winches using grooved drums must include devices that prevent the wire rope from jumping or leaving the assigned groove.

The drums shall be dimensioned in order that a minimum of 3 windings or dead wraps of wire rope remain on the drum at all times.

The diameter of drums and pulleys shall be no less than 30 times the diameter of the wire rope used.

The fleet angle of the wire rope leaving the drum shall be no more than plus or minus 2°.

Wire Ropes

Braided wire ropes and plastic fiber wire ropes are not permitted as load-bearing wire ropes.

Natural and synthetic fiber lines are permitted for use as the principal suspension components only in "hemp" flying systems or in horizontally moved devices. Natural and synthetic fiber lines are not permitted for use as load-bearing lines in winch and counter-weighted flying systems.

Dimensioning of Wire Ropes

The safe working loads of a wire rope shall be determined by dividing the manufacturer's stated breaking strength by the applicable wire rope safety factor.

For horizontally moved technical stage equipment the pulling lines shall be dimensioned with a minimum safety factor of 6.

The strength of the wire rope shall be determined using the following:

LOAD INCREASE FACTORS = 1.25 (or as appropriate)
STRENGTH REDUCTION FACTORS = 0.9 (or as appropriate)

$$\frac{(\text{ULTIMATE STRENGTH})}{(\text{DESIGN LIMIT LOAD})} \times \frac{(\text{STRENGTH REDUCTION FACTORS})}{(\text{LOAD INCREASE FACTORS})}$$

(See "Formula" at the end of the Appendix for further explanation of this formula and its various factors.)

For vertically moved technical stage equipment the wire rope shall be dimensioned with a minimum safety factor of 8.

Attachment of Wire Ropes

Wire ropes shall be attached safely and durably. Installation of attachment devices shall meet manufacturer's specifications.

Wire rope end attached to drums shall be positively secured within the drum.

Slack Line Safety

In motorized vertically moving technical stage equipment, using wire rope wound on drums, a device shall be present that immediately stops the drive when the wire rope becomes slack.

All rigging equipment shall be designed with those appropriate safety and protective measures detailed in section 3 of this Appendix.

5   Machinery Captured in the Stage Floor

In the case of removable- and disassembly-type turntables the safety measures shall be explained in the operations and procedures manual.

Appropriate warning labels shall be permanently attached to the equipment.

The horizontal distance between fixed and movable stage floor surfaces shall not exceed ⅜ in. The vertical distance between fixed and movable floor surfaces shall not exceed ⅛ in.

The movement of captured stage equipment shall be indicated by both audible and visual warning signals. The audible signal may be disabled during performance if the signal interferes with the performance. The visual signal shall remain in operation during all periods of movement.

The visual signals shall be placed in locations so as to be visible to persons endangered by the movement of the equipment.

The visual and audible signals shall be placed at all operating locations.

All personnel including new employees and persons who are temporarily present on the stage shall be instructed in the purpose and the use of the signals. Instructions shall be posted at the stage entrance(s).

Trapdoor covers shall be opened or closed only under the direction of a supervisor. The openings in the stage floor shall be promptly and properly secured when not in use.

Permanent trap covers that are built into the stage floor shall incorporate concealed lifting devices accessible from the stage surface.

Temporary railings and warning signs shall be promptly erected. The railings and warning signs may be removed during performances and rehearsals but shall be replaced promptly upon completion of the rehearsal or performance.

Captured stage machinery may be entered and exited only after instruction from a supervisor; all safety requirements shall be observed with utmost care.

If entry or egress from moving captured stage wagons is required, measures shall be taken to ensure safe footing.

Combustible decorations, scenery, properties, etc., shall not be stored in the trap room or the machinery areas.

Formula

The strength of the wire rope shall be determined using the following:

LOAD INCREASE FACTORS = 1.25 (or as appropriate)
STRENGTH REDUCTION FACTORS = 0.9 (or as appropriate)

$$\frac{(\text{ULTIMATE STRENGTH})}{(\text{DESIGN LIMIT LOAD})} \times \frac{(\text{STRENGTH REDUCTION FACTORS})}{(\text{LOAD INCREASE FACTORS})}$$

Ultimate Strength: The ultimate breaking strength of the wire rope as certified by the manufacturer

Strength Reduction Factors: Those factors that reduce the static load-breaking strength, such as terminating with wire rope clips (.8) or a clove hitch (.65)

Design Limit Load: The weight the wire rope is to lift

Load Increase Factors: Those variable factors that may increase the load above its design limit, such as a curtain absorbing moisture from the atmosphere (1.15), a point load on a batten (1.25), normal motor torque increase (1.5), starting inertia or pulley friction.

Glossary

Act Curtain   Also called FRONT CURTAIN or MAIN CURTAIN. The curtain closest to the proscenium that opens and closes to expose the stage area to the audience.

Apron   The area of the stage that is in front of the proscenium.

Auditorium   The area where the audience is seated. Also called the HOUSE.

Batten   A steel pipe or wooden bar used to support scenery, curtains, and lights. Usually suspended from the grid or roof structure.

Bridge   A movable steel structure suspended over stage or audience area usually used for suspending lighting instruments.

Captured Stage Equipment   Machinery, such as electromechanically or hydraulically driven wagons or turntables, that is part of the structure of the building or is contained in a temporary stage floor.

Catching Device   A protective shield that prevents the system operator from injury should a counterweight become dislodged and fall from the counterweight carriage.

Catwalk   A steel structure over the stage and/or the audience area used by stage personnel to cross from one side to the other.

Controlled Stop   A timed deceleration of a moving device.

Counterweight Carriage   A metal frame that holds the counterweights used to balance the weight of flown scenery. Also referred to as the arbor, cradle, or carriage.

Counterweights   A system of variable weights used to counterbalance loads placed on battens that are moved vertically.

Dead Hung   Battens or similar equipment that is permanently supported from the grid and cannot be easily lowered to the stage floor.

Deflecting Device   Same as CATCHING DEVICE.

Drive Damage   Any event that would impair, alter, or diminish the safe operation of the unit that contains the item.

Expert   A person having extensive training and knowledge in the field of stage rigging and stage machinery.

Reprinted with permission of the United States Institute for Theatre Technology.

Fire Curtain   A nonflammable curtain immediately behind the proscenium, contained in the smoke pocket, used to protect the audience from possible smoke and fire originating from the stage area.

Fly   To move scenery or similar devices vertically on the stage.

Fly Gallery   A platform attached to the side wall of the stage house used to operate the rigging devices.

Fly Loft   The space above the grid and below the roof.

Grid   A steel framework above the stage area used to support the rigging system. Short for GRIDIRON.

Hard Contact   A sudden or uncontrolled stop of the counterweight carriage caused by hitting the upper or lower limits of the system.

Head Block   The first sheave or pulley that is directly above the counterweight carriage or winch with the principal function of changing the direction of travel of the lifting lines from vertical to horizontal.

Hemp System   A system of hemp (now Manila fiber) ropes used to support or raise and lower scenery.

House   See AUDITORIUM.

Loading Gallery   A platform attached to the side walls of the stage house used for the loading or unloading of the counterweight carriages.

Loft Block   The pulleys or sheaves directly above the batten used to change the direction of the working lines from horizontal to vertical.

Motorized Rigging   A system of electric or hydraulic motors used to raise and lower battens or counterweight carriages.

Orchestra Lift   An elevator in the orchestra pit used to raise and lower the floor of the pit.

Pin Rail   A part of a hemp system consisting of a metal pipe or wooden rail attached to the fly gallery and fitted with removable steel or wooden pins used in the tying-off of the working lines.

Pit   A recessed area in front of the stage used principally by musicians. Can also be covered and used as an extended forestage.

Proper Training   Training from a reputable school, college, university, or IATSE local having a formalized apprentice program.

Proscenium   The wall between the stage and the audience containing the proscenium arch.

Rigging   The general term describing systems used to raise and lower or move the stage equipment.

Set   A unit of rigging consisting of the batten and all other support cables, sheaves, and mountings.

Spreader Plates   Movable steel plates on a counterweight arbor used to keep the arbor rods from spreading and counterweights from falling out in case of a sudden stop.

Stage House   That portion of a theatre building containing the stage area, fly loft, grid, and galleries.

Sheave   A grooved wheel in a block or pulley.

Supervisor   A person charged with the responsibility of directing the work of others and the safe operation of stage equipment.

Technical Stage Equipment   A general term indicating the equipment or machinery used on a stage to support the movement of scenery, lighting equipment, or people.

Thrust Stage   An extension of the stage floor into the auditorium, allowing the audience to be seated on three sides.

Traps   Sections of the stage floor that can be removed to access the understage area.

Turntable   A rotating platform or portion of the stage floor.

Winch   A manual or power-operated device used to wind on cable to raise and lower stage equipment.

Wagon   A movable platform usually on casters or wheels.

Well   The space between the beams on the grid over which the loft blocks are placed and the working lines to drop to the batten.

References

American Iron and Steel Institute. *Wire Rope Users Manual.* 2d ed. Washington, D.C.: American Iron and Steel Institute, 1981.

Broderick and Bascom Rope Co. *Riggers Handbook.* St. Louis: Broderick and Bascom, 1975.

Burris-Meyer, Harold, and Edward C. Cole. *Scenery for the Theatre.* Rev. ed. Boston: Little, Brown, 1971.

Crosby Group. *950 General Catalog.* Tulsa: Crosby Group, 1981.

Gillette, A. S. *Stage Scenery.* 2d ed. New York: Harper and Row, 1972.

Macwhyte Co. *Wire Rope Catalog of Tables, Data, and Helpful Information.* Kenosha, Wisc.: 1978.

Newberry, W. G. *Handbook for Riggers.* Calgary, Alberta, Canada.

Parker, W. Oren, and Harvey K. Smith. *Scene Design and Stage Lighting.* 5th ed. New York: Holt, Rinehart and Winston, 1974.

Jay Glerum has worked in professional theatre for over thirty years. He has worked as a stagehand, designed scenery and lighting, taught technical theatre at several universities, consulted on numerous theatre projects, and worked as a systems designer for a major theatre equipment company. He recently coedited the document titled *Recommended Guidelines for Stage Rigging* and *Stage Machinery Specifications and Practices as Developed by the United States Institute for Theatre Technology.*